FLORAL
EVOLUTION

Hardie Grant

BOOKS

FLORAL EVOLUTION

CATHERINE FOXWELL

FLOWERS FOR THE HOME

FLOWERS TO GIVE

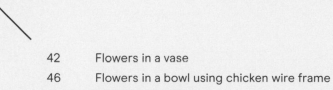

FLOWERS TO WEAR

FLOWERS FOR CELEBRATION

LARGE ARRANGEMENTS

DIY WEDDING FLOWERS

Welcome

I love flowers; it's a fact. Their different shapes, colours and sizes, the element of surprise they provide when they give off an intoxicating smell, and the feelings they evoke in us are like no other. Flowers are there for us in times of joy, sorrow and celebration; there is a place for flowers everywhere.

My floristry journey started around eight years ago when I started taking a few short courses at my local adult education centre. The feedback I received from my teachers was generally good so I started practising more and more in my own time, making a few hand-tied bouquets and doing a little bit of funeral work. In 2014 I decided to bite the bullet and enrolled myself on a part-time City and Guilds diploma in floristry and found myself immersed in the world of flowers even more. At this point I was flooding my mind with every piece of information I could find on flowers and read many floristry books, which were always beautiful to look at although I often thought the flowers featured were not very easy to access or buy for anyone who wasn't a florist.

When I was training I was always conscious of my weekly flower budget for the course – as this wasn't much, I had to be frugal and use more ordinary flowers than I would have liked. I longed for perfect peonies and exotic tropical blooms but these were not accessible and very expensive. It was at this point that I started to explore the beauty of more accessible flowers and, to my surprise, I always managed to create something really nice using flowers that are available to all.

After I finished my course I worked in the industry for a year. I was so lucky to work for some of the best in the business, learning all the time. In October 2016 I decided to set up on my own as Floral Evolution, specialising in weddings and events and the rest is history.

Over the years I have always liked to use flowers that people don't always associate as being trendy or stylish, and this shows in my floristry style, which I would describe as classic with an element of surprise.

I feel that flowers should be accessible to everyone, and in this book I want to show how flowers that are often deemed unpopular or are associated with supermarket bunches can be made into beautiful creations. I will show how you can look for inspiration everywhere, and use sustainable materials to make your arrangements. I want this book to give you the basic tools and techniques to allow your creativity to flourish. When I am running workshops, the first thing I say to attendees is that there is no right or wrong with floristry; it is all about your interpretation of how the materials should work together. I love the fact that although we are all using the same materials in my workshops, every person ends up making something that looks a bit different: that's the beauty of nature; that's the beauty of flowers; that's the beauty of floristry.

I have arranged this book by the different occasions when you may need to create floral designs. It starts with projects on flowers to give, and then leads on to other sections including flowers for your home, for a celebration, and flowers to wear. As a huge part of my business and something I absolutely adore doing is weddings, I have included a whole section on DIY weddings for the brave souls who wish to attempt their wedding flowers themselves.

Taking time to create something with your hands for yourself or for others is a wonderful thing and incredibly rewarding. I get to do this all the time, and I hope that with the easy-to-follow projects in this book you will be able get to do the same.

How to use this book

In this book I have covered all the things that I think you really need to know to be able to tackle most things in floristry, from a hand-tied bouquet to making larger arrangements. It is suitable for anyone who loves flowers, and by following the step-by-step guides in each project I am confident that whatever you make will be beautiful. Many of the materials you will need can be found online, or at floristry or craft suppliers. I have also detailed where to buy your flowers, although many I have used can be purchased from the supermarket or can be grown in the garden or in containers.

I have really focused on making beautiful floral designs with flowers that you are likely to be able to buy easily, and which are not too expensive. I have also concentrated on keeping the materials and vessels needed for the majority of the projects to only a few, to show how you can reuse them in different settings.

Each chapter starts with the project that uses the most flower content, and then the following projects in the chapter show you how to get the most out of the materials as flowers fade and eventually come to the end of their life. The projects are very straightforward and – as flowers are a visual thing – looking at the pictures first will give you a good idea about whether you can just dive in and have a go, or if you need read up on the instructions before you start. There are a few larger projects that are a little bit more complex and may take a bit longer, but nothing in this book is very hard when you are equipped with knowledge, skills and the right techniques. Please use my instructions as a guide and have fun experimenting with different flowers and foliage than those suggested. I have chosen materials that can be purchased all year round, but have included a section on my favourite seasonal flowers and where it's best to buy them.

I also wanted to explore the beauty of individual flowers, so I take a closer look at the lifespan of flowers and how you can change the look and shape of them. I also touch on how, when the fresh stage has finished, you can get even more out of them when dried.

I believe that practise makes perfect, and I have included lots of tips and techniques on floristry basics. This will give you the foundation you need to explore your own creativity, and ultimately find your own floral style. Floristry has no real rules, and I hope that this book will show that you don't need to spend huge amounts of money to make something stunning, special and unique.

As I am a wedding and event florist, I had to write a section on doing your own wedding flowers. As with any profession, you hire a florist to make sure that you will have the best and most beautiful flowers for your wedding. A florist will have access to a wide choice of flowers, will know when to buy them to make sure they look their absolute best on the day, and they will offer ideas and options to get the most out of your budget. They will also do all the organisation with your venue, taking the pressure off you, saving you time and giving you peace of mind. Florists are the experts in their field, with experience and years of training. That is what you pay for. But if you want to do your flowers yourself, all you need is the creativity, time and passion to undertake this task. You will definitely need help, so make sure you have friends and family on board to assist, and of course to make the tea when things are getting a bit stressful.

The key things for success are planning, time and delivery – and this applies to doing flowers for other big events too. Do your homework: check what flowers are in season at the time of the wedding, what flowers you like, and research where you can buy them. Write down everything you need to make and calculate the volumes you need, remembering to order a few extra stems to allow for breakages. It will help if you split your wedding flowers into bridal flowers and venue flowers, and keep them separate when they arrive so that you don't mix them up. You also need to consider the other items you will need like vases, urns and support materials. Finally, you will have to arrange access and delivery times with your venue, so you know the timescales you will be working to. In some cases you might be allowed to set up the night before, taking off some of the pressure on the day of your wedding. Use everyone who is willing to help you, and give your helpers specific tasks so things run to plan.

You will need time to get everything ready and space to store everything. I have done many weddings, and everything always takes longer than you think it will. Flowers arrive in their raw state and need be conditioned as explained on page 32, placed in fresh water and stored in a nice cool place – you'll need lots of buckets. You will need to consider when to buy each flower type. A Rose will take a few days to open up to full bloom, but a Sweet Pea will only last a few days so is ideally bought later. Stored flowers will need stems recut and the water changed every few days. Timing is key in this process: venue flowers can be made up to three days before the wedding and bridal up to two days before. The day before the wedding, check all the flowers and replace any that look tired or have wilted.

Now all the hard work is done, the flowers are made, you are over the moon with the results and everything is ready to go. The last thing to do is to make sure the delivery and set-up goes smoothly and without a hitch. Keep in touch with the venue, know the exact time you are allowed to deliver and make sure that you have a car big enough for transporting the arrangements and a suitable method to transport them safely. The last thing you want it is for all your hard work to be destroyed if arrangements aren't packed securely for delivery. Use bubble wrap or paper to keep things in place and take time to pack the arrangements carefully so stems aren't broken.

I applaud anybody who takes on this task, but if you plan everything carefully you will be amazed with what can be achieved. Many of the arrangements in this book can be used for a wedding, but the final chapter covers some wedding essentials.

Tools and equipment

Here is a list of essential tools that you will need to create the arrangements in this book. For the three larger arrangements you will need some extra equipment, but this is listed in that specific project.

SCISSORS *fig. a*

If you are going to do a lot of floristry, I recommend investing in a pair of carbon blade scissors, which are super sharp and last a very long time. If you are not, it is still worth buying a decent pair of floristry scissors. The ones with yellow handles are very good. The reason a lot of floristry equipment has bright coloured handles is to make sure you can find them if they are buried in a mound of foliage.

SECATEURS *fig. b*

A good pair of garden secateurs really comes into its own if you are cutting woody stems or larger branches. Secateurs are particularly good when you are foraging.

fig. l

fig. j

fig. f

fig. e

fig. m

fig. i

fig. k

fig. c

fig. b

fig. d

fig. g

fig. a

fig. h

WIRE CUTTERS *fig. c*

As you will be using chicken wire in this book, and may need to cut floristry wires if you are going to attempt wiring flowers, I highly recommend buying some wire cutters. Cutting wire with scissors will make them blunt so try not to use them if at all possible.

CHICKEN WIRE *fig. d*

Throughout this book I have used chicken wire as the mechanic for holding stems in place. Chicken wire is really easy to make into the shape you desire and can be found online or in most hardware stores. The holes in the wire should be around 5 cm (2 in) in diameter – you can make them smaller to hold your stems by overlapping the wire or by squashing the wire into a ball.

FLORISTS' POT TAPE *fig. e*

This tape can be bought at wholesale suppliers or online and is really great for making sure all your chicken wire is held securely in its vessels. It is waterproof, really sticky and I love using it to tape my bridal bouquets instead of tying with string. It's also useful to hold stems in place as you are building the bouquet by wrapping the tape round them.

GREEN FLORISTS' STEM TAPE *fig. f*

Used for wiring, you can buy a paper tape or a waterproof tape. I find the paper tape easier to use but both work well.

STRING *fig. g*

Essential for tying any type of bouquet.

FLOWER FROG OR KENZAN *fig. h*

This can also be called a pin holder. It consists of a heavy lead plate with a number of spikes that are used to hold stems in place in a similar way to chicken wire. These are becoming increasingly popular in place of chicken wire and I know lots of florists who use both as extra security to hold stems in place. The flower frog is also ideal for practising Ikebana minimal-style arrangements – an example of how to make this style of arrangement is on page 54.

OASIS FIX ADHESIVE TACK *fig. i*

Waterproof sticky putty is used to secure a flower frog or kenzan to the bottom of the vessel. When placing your frog and putty in the vessel, make sure it is dry at the time of fixing before filling with water.

CABLE TIES *fig. j*

For your larger creations you will need cable ties to secure the chicken wire in place. A mixed bag from any DIY store with different lengths and thicknesses is best.

FLORAL WATER TUBES *fig. k*

I use these to provide a water source for flowers when they cannot drink directly from a vessel. These tubes can be purchased online, or if you buy flowers like Anthurium they come with their own tubes that can then be saved for when you need them.

FLORISTS' WIRES *fig. l*

A selection of florists' wires is useful to have, especially for wired work. The lower the gauge, the finer the wire so a 22-gauge wire is thinner than an 18-gauge wire.

REEL WIRE *fig. m*

I have used this wire a lot in this book as it can be purchased easily and is wonderful for all different types of projects. It is great for making garlands and wreaths and you can get away with using it to make larger or dried flower crowns.

Other useful extras

BUCKETS AND CONTAINERS

You will need buckets to store your flowers in. Recycled bottles, tubs and any other containers can be used when you need to make larger installations.

KNIFE

A floristry knife is handy for conditioning flowers – I like to use a knife to strip thorns from the stems of roses.

LAZY SUSAN

This is good for making table arrangements as it allows you to turn your arrangement to view it from all sides. If you are going to make lots of table centres, buying one would be a good investment.

SMALL RIBBON-CUTTING SCISSORS

It's best to keep a separate pair of scissors for cutting ribbon. Your floristry scissors will not do a great job of cutting material, and no one wants to see ribbon featuring green stains.

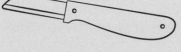

A WORD ON FLORAL FOAM

In this book I have not used floral foam for any of the projects. This is because there are so many sustainable alternatives to foam and half the fun of floristry is working out the mechanics needed to support your design. Floral foam is no doubt a very useful thing, and there is nothing to stop you from using it, but as it isn't biodegradable it sadly ends up in landfill. Using chicken wire, flower frogs and any other clever mechanics that you may dream up are a better alternative to floral foam, and I for one want to do what I can to practise environmentally friendly, sustainable floristry.

Vessels

This book is all about accessibility, keeping things simple and yet achieving amazing, beautiful and interesting designs.

With this in mind, I have decided to recommend a capsule wardrobe-style number of vessels that you will need to make all the arrangements and designs in this book. The vessel you use for your arrangements is really important as it will have an overall effect on the final design. I think these six vessels are enough to get you started, and then as your style develops you can add more vessels to your collection. It can become a very enjoyable part of floral design; just make sure you have enough room to store all your goodies.

You don't have to spend lots of money on vessels. Online auctions, charity shops and car boot sales are often treasure troves for many beautiful individual special items.

SMALL BOWL *fig. a*

A small ceramic bowl is great for making small low arrangements using just a few ingredients.

LONG AND LOW TROUGH STYLE VASE *fig. b*

These are really useful for making an arrangement that runs down the middle of a table, or for a mantlepiece arrangement.

FOOTED BOWL *fig. c*

This is my favourite shaped vessel. With its shallow wide neck and added height, it is perfect for asymmetrical arrangements that allow for some of the materials to flow over the edge of the bowl onto the table.

GLASS CYLINDER VASE *fig. d*

A lovely wide glass cylinder vase is always useful. One around 15 cm (6 in) wide is perfect for your hand-tied bouquets.

BUD VASE *fig. e*

The ideal vessel for when your large bunch of flowers becomes smaller and smaller as blooms fade away. The bud vase is a wonderful way of displaying simple stems and allows you to really appreciate the true beauty of individual flowers. Bottles can also be used as bud vases as they have a narrow neck.

LARGE URN *fig. f*

If you are going to make larger arrangements for events, then investing in a large urn will allow you to make stand-out designs. While they are quite a traditional vessel, they are good because they add height and drama to any arrangement and allow for materials to drape over the edge, similar to the footed bowl.

fig. d

fig. f

fig. c

fig. b

fig. a

fig. e

Buying and sourcing flowers

There are many different places that you can buy flowers and I am always so happy to see a wide range of seasonal flowers on offer in more places. This means you can enjoy a mix of colours, varieties and smells all year round. In this book I have focused on accessibility and cost as the main factors to show how you can make something beautiful with easy-to-purchase flowers. Here are the main places that you can purchase flowers and some things you should be aware of when making that all important decision on where to buy.

SUPERMARKETS

Supermarkets have a good source of flowers that are normally available all year round. I am really pleased to see that more seasonal offerings, which are often locally grown, are also being made available. Seasonal flowers are normally stocked in larger stores, so it may be worthwhile making a special trip if you are looking for something that hasn't had as far to travel to end up in your shopping basket.

LOCAL FLORIST SHOPS

Your local florist shop will offer a much wider range of flowers than a supermarket, and you should be able to get some seasonal offerings. Most flowers that you see in the florists will be received from Dutch auctions, and many Roses come from much further afield, like Ecuador and Kenya. Some of these flowers may be locally sourced but the majority will have had to travel.

LOCAL FLOWER MARKETS

There is nothing quite like the buzz and intoxicating smell of the local flower market. In London we are very lucky to have New Covent Garden flower market, where there is an array of imported flowers, plants and a good selection of home-grown seasonal flowers and foliage. The flower market is open to both trade and non-trade customers and I always suggest that you go there with a bit of an idea of what you wish to buy. Be ready to set your alarm early as most of the goodies can be gone by 7 am in the morning; I find between 5 and 6 am is a good time to visit as there is normally a good selection available. When you buy directly at wholesale the quantities are large – they are normally in wraps of 10s, 20s, 25s and 50s. The price can be eye-wateringly expensive when you are buying such large quantities, plus don't forget VAT is an additional charge. A great way to reduce this cost is by visiting the market with a friend, splitting the cost of the flowers and having a wonderful breakfast at the market café before you leave. What a great start to any day.

YOUR GARDEN

If you are lucky enough to have a garden to grow your own flowers, then picking something you have grown from either bulb or seed is extremely rewarding. When cutting from a garden the best time is either first thing in the morning or at dusk in the evening; these times are when the stems are full of water. Always place your cut stems straight into a bucket of water and keep them in there until you are ready to make your creations.

FLOWER FARMS AND LOCAL GROWERS

Due to increased pressures on imported flowers and costs, local growers are coming into their own. They provide flowers that have a bit of interest and are mostly seasonal. You can look online to see if there are any growers nearby, and many sell buckets of blooms or allow you to pick your own. I recently went to a local flower farm near where I live in London and it was a joyous occasion. Being able to pick my own flowers was simply amazing and the imperfect, interesting stems that add that something special to your arrangements were available in abundance. It is so wonderful to support local growers, and if you have time, spending a morning picking your own blooms is, to me, like spending a day being pampered at a spa.

FORAGING

I like to forage a few stems of foliage as they often add wonderful texture and interest that make arrangements sing. There are some rules with foraging that are really important to follow. Never cut stems from a Royal Park because it is illegal and you could be prosecuted. Always ask permission if you wish to cut from a neighbour's garden or a bush that is overhanging the road. Nine times out of ten permission will be given, but please make sure that you don't destroy the plant and only cut what you need. Always forage sensitively, making a clean cut at the bottom of the stem. Once you have foraged your stems it goes without saying that you should put them straight into a clean bucket of water as they will need a good drink before arranging.

My favourite seasonal flowers

This book concentrates on accessible flowers that you will be able to buy all year round, but seasonal flowers cannot be ignored. There really is nothing better than seasonal flowers; like food, flowers that are meant to be available at a certain point in the year will always be at their best, and in a lot of ways this makes them so special.

I would urge you to experiment with the best of the season, even if you can only afford a few seasonal stars to add to the more accessible flowers. I feel they can really elevate an arrangement to another level.

Some flowers, like Ranunculus, will span a couple of seasons – first appearing in winter and finishing late spring. That's when you have the magic of maybe having your favourite flowers available in the same month. Here are some of my seasonal stars, which I have listed in the season when they are at their very best. I am sure that many are or may become your favourites too.

SPRING

The time when everything starts to awaken and flowering bulbs take centre stage.

Anemone

Cherry Blossom

Clematis

Daffodil

Fritillaria

Hyacinth

Lilac

Muscari

Ranunculus

Tulip

SUMMER

The time when showy, blousy, abundant blooms are everywhere to be seen.

Astrantia

Cornflower

Cosmos

Foxglove

Japanese Anemone

Lupin

Peony

Rose

Sweet Pea

Sunflower

AUTUMN

The time when everything starts to turn, and rich tones of reds and oranges come into their own.

Achillea

Amaranthus

Blackberry

Cotinus

Crocosmia

Dahlia

Helinium

Hydrangea

Nerine

Zinnia

WINTER

The time for delicate flowers in pale shades of white and seasonal foliage in many shades of green.

Amaryllis

Camellia

Cyclamen

Hellebore

Magnolia

Mimosa

Muscari

Salix

Snowdrop

Viburnum

I have detailed on pages 16–17 some of the best places you can buy seasonal flowers, and if you have any outdoor space or a garden you can try growing some yourself.

Basic support methods

When you are learning floristry and mastering techniques there are some useful basic methods that will help you throughout your journey. One of the trickiest parts of floristry is working out the best mechanics to support your design. When deciding you need to consider the following: can it be made in place (for instance, a flower arch may be set up at the venue); will you need to transport it; what size will it be; is there a place to hang things from (for larger and hanging arrangements). Here are some of the methods used in the book in more detail, plus a few extra techniques that I think are really useful to know. It is a good idea to look though this section before embarking on the projects.

Chicken wire in a bowl, trough or footed bowl

This method is great for any vessel because the chicken wire can be re-used and manipulated into any shape. It is a great way of securing your flower materials in place with ease.

MATERIALS

vessel of choice

chicken wire

wire cutters

florists' pot tape

STEP 1

Select your vessel of choice.

STEP 2

Cut your chicken wire to size – a good guide is around twice the circumference of the vessel. This may need adjustment, dependant on the materials you use because you will need less if your materials have thicker stems.

STEP 3

Loosely squash the wire into a ball shape, or whatever shape it needs to be to fit your chosen vessel. Once the wire is in place, make sure it is about 1 cm (⅜ in) higher than the edge of the vessel.

STEP 4

Tape the chicken wire into place with pot tape. I like to form a cross with the tape and then place the tape around the circumference of the vessel, making sure it covers the edges of the cross.

STEP 5

Add water to your vessel until it is around three-quarters full – never fill to the brim. If you are transporting the arrangement, you can always top it up when it's in place. Now the hard work is done, it is time to have fun making your arrangement.

Grid method

If you are making an arrangement in a glass vase and do not want any chicken wire to show, this method works very well. Making a grid across the top of the vase allows for stems to be supported, but is invisible through the glass.

MATERIALS

> glass vase
>
> florists' pot tape

STEP 1

> Make sure the vase is completely dry before attaching the tape. This is important as if it is at all damp the tape will not attach to the glass properly.

STEP 2

> Cut strands of tape and secure them across the opening of the vase. Place them equally spaced out, first one way and then at right angles to create a grid. Each square on average should be around 2 cm (¾ in) but again this will differ if you are making an arrangement with thicker stems.

STEP 3

> Use a small watering can to fill the vase through one of the holes until it is around three-quarters full.

STEP 4

> Start placing your flowers and foliage through the holes, with the grid doing its job of holding them in place.

Flower frog/ kenzan

This method is most used in minimal Ikebana style arrangements, with only a few stems. However, it can also be used for larger free-form arrangements. If your creation is going to be really flower heavy, add in some chicken wire for extra support.

MATERIALS

> vessel of choice
>
> flower frog
>
> oasis fix adhesive tack

STEP 1

> Take the adhesive tack and lay a ring around the base of the frog, making sure it overlaps the edge of the base by about 2 mm. This is a tip from a wonderful florist who uses flower frogs for all her arrangements and it really helps to keep the frog in place.

STEP 2

> Twist your frog into place, making sure it is securely fixed.

STEP 3

> Fill your vase with water until all the spikes of the frog are covered and begin arranging your flowers. When using a flower frog for a more abundant arrangement, always start with the heavier materials first and build up from there.

Basic wiring techniques

MATERIALS

range of wires from 20s–28-gauge

flowers or leaves of choice

florists' stem tape, either paper or waterproof

wire cutters

I have covered wiring using dried flowers in some detail (pages 86–89) as it is an easy introduction to mastering this technique. However, if you fancy giving wiring with fresh flowers a go to create flower crowns, buttonholes and corsages, here are some tips on how to wire some commonly-used flowers and foliage. Wiring flowers takes practise and patience. The wire replaces bulky stems, allowing you to manipulate a flower or leaf into a desired shape. I don't normally wire my buttonholes as I make them like mini bouquets to allow greater variation, but corsages need to be wired because they are normally attached to light-weight ladies' dresses so need to be as delicate as possible. See page 76 for how to make a fresh flower corsage. You will need to use a thin wire as you don't want bulky wires showing in your work. Around a 26-gauge wire is a good choice. Taping the stems helps to retain moisture as the stems are out of water. Once you have made your wired work, lightly spray it with water and place in a cold place like a refrigerator until the items are needed.

Roses

STEP 1

Cut the stem, leaving about 1 cm (⅜ in).

STEP 2

I like to place a heavier 20-gauge wire up the middle of the stem for extra support. Then take a finer wire, around 26-gauge, and push it just under the head of the Rose from one side to the other. Wrap the wire several times around the stem and down around the heavier wire.

STEP 3

Trim the wires and cover with stem tape, remembering to stretch and pull it down the stem. To make sure the stem tape is ready for use, I like to put it in my pocket around 30 minutes before use to warm it up – this helps it to stick to the stem. The tape is also easier to stretch when it is warmed up.

Leaves

STEP 1

Cut the stem leaving around 1–2 cm (³⁄₈–³⁄₄ in).

STEP 2

Turn the leaf face down and insert a fine wire through the central vein from side to side (like making a stitch) around two thirds down the leaf. Bend the ends of the wire down, forming a loop to create a support, and then twist the wires around the base of the leaf.

STEP 3

Cover the wire with florists' stem tape.

Buds

To support tiny buds, which are really nice when included in a corsage, use a fine 26-gauge or lighter wire. Push the wire just below the petals into the calyx and twist down the stem. Cover the wire with florists' stem tape.

Other flowers

For most other flowers you can either form a loop on the base of the remaining stem and tape, or for flowers that last well out of water like Lisianthus push a wire through the area just below the petals, wind down the remaining stem and cover with stem tape.

Principles and elements of design

This may seem like a really old-fashioned term but knowing the principles and elements of flower design will help you to tackle any type of arrangement. These considerations are worth thinking about, but are not ones to dwell on as creativity comes from the heart and rules can sometimes stifle this. As I was traditionally trained at college, I do often think about the principles and elements of design and how they are really challenged in modern floristry – in a good way. Here are some basic tips to help you on your way with making your arrangements. Practise, experiment and have fun with flowers and all of these principles will become something you won't even have to think about – they will just become flower-arranging habit.

Colour

When I was learning all about flowers we used the colour wheel as a visual tool to help make decisions on what colours go well together. It is something I refer to still because it really helps to picture how colours will work with each other. In today's world of floristry colour combinations are pushed to new limits, but I still feel that the colour wheel does somehow underpin these choices, however experimental they may be.

The wheel is a circle of 12 full-strength colours designed to show the natural associations between colours. It starts with the three primary colours – red, yellow and blue. Any two of these can be mixed together to make a secondary colour: yellow and blue make green; yellow and red make orange; red and blue make violet. The final tertiary colours are produced by mixing a primary colour with an adjacent secondary colour – for example blue

and green make blue-green. Neutral colours – white, black and grey – are not technically colours, they are added to change a colour to produce a different tone or shade.

So how do we use the wheel? I like to use it to see which colours complement each other – so colours that are next to each other on the wheel – or for a more vibrant clashing combination the ones that are opposite each other.

A colour scheme will often be determined by the event or occasion you are making flowers for, but using the following colour harmonies may help you to decide on which colours will be better placed together.

MONOCHROMATIC

'Mono' means 'single', so this uses one hue from the colour wheel and variation is achieved by using different tints, tones and shades of the same colour.

ANALOGOUS

This is where you use a primary colour and incorporate adjacent colours, so red is incorporated with different shades of red and red-violet. This produces a rich, interesting colour palette.

SPLIT COMPLEMENTARY

These are colours from opposite sides of the colour wheel, which often results in an unexpected harmonious colour combination.

COMPLEMENTARY

Tints, tones and shades of a chosen colour make a complementary colour palette. This could be different shades of pinks, lilacs and neutral shades of white and it results in a harmonious palette being achieved.

CONTRAST

Yellow and blue have no relationship with each other on the colour wheel, but combining two primary colours produces a wonderfully vibrant colour combination.

POLYCHROMATIC

This colour harmony is where you use as many colours as you wish from the colour wheel – a combination that is used in many Dutch master paintings. Much inspiration can be drawn from these wonderful examples, where a mash up of colours results in something rather exciting being made.

WARM AND COLD COLOURS

Some colours evoke warm, cosy feelings and moods, and others create a colder, clinical feel. This is the case with flowers, too. An arrangement of vivid pink Peonies, orange and yellow Roses and peach Lisianthus will feel much warmer than an arrangement of blue Delphinium, Nigella and white Roses. Remember that flowers evoke feelings and this must be considered when making your colour choices.

I hope this whistle-stop tour on colour gives you food for thought. I would always say: take time to read the theory behind colour choice and then use this to make up your own rules, as there is definitely no right or wrong in my opinion.

Basic design considerations

There are some design elements that you may wish to consider when making your arrangements. Floral design can be divided into four basic principles, which are: form; lines; focal point; recession. Scale and proportion and visual and actual balance are also important to know about when tackling a floral design. With every design you make, it's worth thinking about these basic considerations.

FORM

This is the outline of your design – form decides how high and wide your arrangement will be and remember it is good to consider three dimension in any design as you do not want your arrangement to look flat. Focal, line, filler flowers and foliage often inform the form of a design, see page 39.

FOCAL POINT, LINE AND RECESSION

A focal point is needed in a design because it draws the eye to a certain point, while the lines made with your flowers allow the eye to travel through the design. I often use a couple of larger focal flowers to achieve a focal point, with smaller similar flowers providing a line or path for the eye to reach the focal point. A group of flowers can also provide a focal point, while using similar flowers dug in or recessed into the arrangement will give your designs depth and dimension.

SCALE AND PROPORTION

Very early on in my floristry journey, while training at college, I made a corsage using the most enormous Gerbera. I had the sense to notice that this was far too huge to be worn nicely and this made me think about choosing the right-sized materials, and making sure they were the correct scale and proportion.

Scale is really important to think about when making any flower design. I normally use the rule of thirds, and this is a pretty good principle for most type of floral design. When making a hand-tied bouquet the rule is normally two-thirds flower and one-third stem. This goes for an arrangement in a vase or in a footed bowl, too. When thinking about scale and proportion I think of extremes – you wouldn't want to make an adult-sized bridesmaid's bouquet for a five-year-old flower girl. Keep these thoughts in mind and you will find that you make the right choices for any occasion very quickly.

A good example of scale.

ACTUAL AND VISUAL BALANCE

Any arrangement you make will need actual balance so it will be able to stand upright without toppling over in any direction. This is achieved by making sure that the materials are balanced throughout the arrangement, and an even distribution of weight is applied when making up the arrangement. This principle goes for any type of flower arrangement – you cannot have a mass of really heavy-headed flowers like Lilies on one side of an arrangement or bouquet, and Gerberas on the other; it just won't work and will result in a pool of water on the floor where the arrangement has tipped over. This will take some practise, but always keep in mind that even distribution is key to any successful arrangement.

Visual balance is far more difficult to achieve than actual balance. For an arrangement to really work and have visual balance, it will have a focal point. Darker colours to the middle of the design and lighter ones to the edges. Lighter detail elements, like grasses and floating foliage, to the edges and larger elements in the middle. Some elements dug in and recessed give weight and dimension to the design.

Good use of colour is also important in achieving visual balance; more concentration of colour in the middle of the arrangement will give the arrangement depth and visual weight while paler, lighter colours can be used on the outer edges of the design.

A poor example of scale.

Conditioning and care

So, you have bought all your flowers and foliage but before you arrange them you must do one of the most important parts of floristry – and that is condition them. Conditioning flowers and foliage will help them last as long as possible and look their best for longer.

Conditioning first involves taking off all the lower leaves that will sit below the water level in a vase or arrangement – or if you're making a hand-tied bouquet leaves must be stripped below the binding point where you tie the bouquet. As with cutting a stem too short you cannot put leaves back, so make sure you remove them gradually, working from bottom to top. You don't always need to take off lots of leaves, especially if you want to make a more natural loose arrangement or bouquet – the leaves can help to make the arrangement look fuller. The reason we take the leaves off is because if they are left under the water they will contaminate it with bacteria, which makes the vase life of your flowers shorter.

Once the leaves have been removed, the next step is to cut the stem at a diagonal to make sure that it has the largest surface area to take up water. Whenever you buy any flowers and foliage always recut the stems. When you place the recut stems into fresh water it's like

the flowers are drawing breath and consuming all the goodness they need to survive.

If you purchase a multi-headed flower or piece of foliage that has several branches, you can sectional cut them to get the most value out of them. An example of this is a Lisianthus, which has multiple stems that you can cut to make separate stems. Always do this at the lowest point of the stem to allow it to be used in more things; the longer the stem the better, as you can always cut it down for the intended purpose.

Make sure you place any flowers in clean fresh water and a clean vase. If you can, try and change the water every few days, cutting a small section off the stems each time. Purchased bunches of flowers may come with a sachet of flower food and I see no harm in using it. However, clean fresh water in a clean vessel is, in my opinion, all flowers and foliage need to make them last as long as possible.

How long should flowers last?

This is the million-dollar question. It is so dependent on the flowers in the arrangement and how well you look after them. A Carnation can last as long as two weeks – maybe longer – but a spring flower may only last a few days. I think that this is the beauty of flowers; the fleeting life and pleasure a beautiful unusual stem brings at that moment is one to be treasured, and as it fades away we must not be sad – we must remember that some flowers are there just for a small time, making them all the more special.

As a florist, one of the most important jobs is keeping the flowers and foliage in the best condition possible. By following these techniques you will be just like us in caring for your flowers to make sure you get the absolute best out of them.

Tips and tricks for certain flowers

CARNATIONS

These favourites of mine often arrive in tight bud. The flowers are quite hardy and can take a bit of manipulation. With a bit of care, you can brush the firm petals open with your hands. Do avoid any Carnations if the petals are soft and curling inwards with the stamens showing, because this means the flower is past its best.

LILIES

If you purchase Lilies fully open this means that they are in the later stages of their lives. Lilies in bud have sometimes been kept in cold storage but their tight buds trick you into thinking they are fresh. Look out for wilting leaves because this is a clue that they could be older than you think. Remember Lilies can take a very long time to open – sometimes a few weeks – so if you need them open for an event do make sure you buy them in early.

SUMMER FLOWERS

Summer blooms like Stocks, Dahlias and Delphiniums have soft stems that don't last as long in water as some other blooms, such as a Carnation. To make sure the blooms last it is important to change the water regularly to stop the stems getting really slimy.

Releasing flowers from captivity

Bought flower bunches are normally wrapped in cellophane, which can be very bad for the flowers because if they are stored like this in damp conditions it can result in the flowers becoming floppy and wilting. If you spot a bunch where there a few brown petals, do avoid it. The exception is Tulips, which benefit from being left wrapped in paper until they have been conditioned in water for a few hours. For all other flowers I suggest you remove them fully from the cellophane and any bindings as soon as you get your flowers home, to allow air to circulate freely between the blooms while they are having a good drink of water.

An example of how to sectional cut a flower. See page 32 for further information.

Revival techniques

Flowers can be tricky customers, and sometimes the more commonly used flowers, such as Roses, Tulips, Gerbera and Hydrangeas, can be sensitive and hang their heads – leaving you with a less than impressive bunch of flowers. However, there is a quick way to revive them. Take several pieces of newspaper that are strong enough to support the flower heads. Lay the flowers flat on the paper and roll it around them so that any drooping heads are held totally upright. Re-cut the stems at a diagonal, then plunge the bundle into deep water and leave for a few hours to drink. When you unwrap the bundle the flowers should be fully revived and looking much healthier than before.

Flowers and foliage that last well out of water

There are some occasions when you need to use flowers and foliage that will survive for some time without a source of water – for instance, when you are creating an arch or when you are making bridal flowers like buttonholes and corsages.

When flowers and foliage are conditioned properly and have had a good drink beforehand (page 32), many can survive a number of hours without a water source. Here are some that do particularly well:

FLOWERS

Anthurium

Carnations (spray and bloom)

Chrysanthemums (spray and bloom)

Lilies

Limonium

Lisianthus

Orchids

Spray roses

Thistles

FOLIAGE

Conifer (pine, spruce)

Eucalyptus

Ivy

Magnolia

Monstera leaves

Palm leaves

Ruscus

Shapes and forms of flowers

Flowers in any arrangement have a major part to play, which is why they come in so many different shapes and forms, which help to create magical arrangements. In this book I will refer to different types of flowers as line, focal or filler. These terms are explained in more detail here.

FOCAL FLOWERS *fig. a*

These are the stars of the show – the flower that catches your attention and stops you in your tracks. It is always a good idea to include a focal flower in your arrangements, something special that draws your eye. These flowers tend to be round in shape and are large single-headed blooms. Some of my favourite focal flowers are Roses of any description, especially garden Roses, as well as Peonies and Dahlias.

SECONDARY FLOWERS *fig. b*

I like to think of as these flowers as the bridesmaids to the bride – the supporting act but beautiful in their own right. They tend to have a slightly different shape to the focal flowers but are ordinarily a single-stemmed flower. A smaller Rose or a Lisianthus is a good example of this flower type.

FILLER FLOWERS *fig. c*

This flower type is hugely important to any flower arrangement. Filler flowers tend to be multiheaded, dainty and a bit bushy, which adds depth, and they are super useful for filling in any gaps you may have in your arrangements. My favourite filler flowers are Wax Flower and Astrantia, which are more difficult to buy – a more common filler flower is Gypsophila.

LINE FLOWERS *fig. d*

These flowers come into their own when you need to add height or interest to a flower arrangement. They work really well for a dramatic hand-tied bouquet and are great for large arrangements, to help define line and shape. I love Snapdragons and Delphiniums most as line flowers, but if you can't get hold of them, foliage can take on the same role.

TEXTURE *fig. e*

Thistles, Poppy seed heads, dried flowers and grasses bring texture to an arrangement. They are the tiny details that add a little element of surprise.

FOLIAGE *fig. f*

If your preference is to make more wild arrangements, then foliage will play a huge part. A balance of something green in flower design is important because it provides a neutral backdrop for the flowers to shine against. Sometimes you will like your arrangements to be more flower heavy and abundant – in these instances only a small amount of foliage is needed. I like to use small leaves in my flower designs, and I have no problem with them looking a little mottled and weathered. I think this brings a sense of honesty and depth to any type of flower arrangement you will make.

FLOWERS
FOR

THE
HOME

What could be nicer than walking into your home to be greeted by a beautiful bunch of flowers in your favourite vase. Flowers have a way of lifting people's mood and can add a special something to any home. I believe everyone should have access to the joy flowers bring to a home, and this section explores how you can get the most out of accessible flowers by showing three designs using the same flowers in different ways. We start with a vase arrangement that will have the most flowers. As flowers die off and your bunch gets smaller, there are some different options to try with the remaining flowers.

Flowers are such a versatile thing and offer so many possibilities. When I was training to be a florist, my college teacher always instilled in me that there is no right or wrong with creativity, so my words to you are to have a go, enjoy your arrangements, and experiment, as there is so much fun to be had.

Flowers in a vase

For a vase arrangement it is good to have a nice mixture of focal, filler and line flowers, so I suggest buying single-flower bunches and combining them rather than buying a mixed bunch of flowers. The ingredients detailed below are a guide only and you may need more or fewer flowers depending on the size of your vase.

FLOWERS AND FOLIAGE

some greenery from your garden, foraged or purchased from your local florist

5 Stocks

5 Roses

5 Alstroemeria

5 Lisianthus

5 Carnation blooms

3 spray Chrysanthemums

OTHER ITEMS

your favourite vase

florists' scissors or secateurs

support material of your choice (optional)

See guide to support mechanisms on pages 20.

Step 1

Check that your vase is really clean and then prepare it using one of the methods on pages 22–23. Condition all your flowers and foliage as on pages 32.

Step 2

Start with the foliage, making a framework for your flowers to sit in. If you haven't added a support mechanism to your vase, simply criss crossing the foliage stems works really well.

Step 3

Place three of your Stocks or other line flowers in first, then add in a few Roses (focal flower) and then a few stems of Alstroemeria (filler flower). Make sure everything is nicely spaced out.

Step 4

Continue to add in flowers, grouping them if you wish, and allowing space between each bloom until you have used all your flowers and are happy with where they are sitting.

Step 5

Finish by setting your gorgeous arrangement in the place that will bring you the most joy.

Flowers in a bowl using chicken wire frame

I like to experiment with different forms, shapes and styles using vessels that I already have in my home. I have made lots of arrangements in a bowl and I find it one of the easiest and nicest ways to use chicken wire, especially if you are new to using this material when arranging flowers. The chicken wire provides a frame in your bowl so the flowers and foliage stay in the right place. I normally use a small pasta bowl for this style of arrangement but feel free to use any bowl of choice. I prefer to make my arrangements asymmetrical with one side higher than the other, but you can make a bowl arrangement in any style you wish. It is nice with these designs to allow space in between your flowers and foliage, which means each flower can be appreciated and admired.

FLOWERS AND FOLIAGE

some greenery from your garden, foraged or purchased from your local florist

5 Roses

3 Stocks

3 Lisianthus

3 Carnation blooms

3 Alstroemeria

2 spray Chrysanthemums

OTHER ITEMS

a small bowl measuring around 15 cm (6 in) diameter; the larger your bowl the more material you will need

chicken wire

wire cutters

florists' pot tape

florists' scissors or secateurs

Step 1

Make sure your bowl is really clean, then follow instructions on page 22 to add the chicken wire. Fill two thirds full with water when the chicken wire is in place.

Step 2

Make sure all your stems have been recut and are ready for arranging.

Step 3

Start with your foliage. Place three pieces of foliage in your bowl, one tall piece to either the left or right, one in the middle and one slightly overhanging the edge. The tall piece will normally be two-thirds higher than the height of your bowl as a guide.

Step 4

Place three of the Roses, following the placements of the foliage at varying heights for interest.

Step 5

Next fill in the gaps with your line flower, in this case Stocks, keeping one side higher than the other like your foliage placements. Remember to turn your arrangement to work on all sides, which can be done on a lazy Susan (see equipment page 13) – or if you don't have one of these you can just turn your arrangement round yourself.

Step 6

Continue to add in flowers, varying the height and spacing them in the chicken wire frame until you have used all your flowers and are happy with where they are sitting. If there are gaps in your arrangement it is fine to leave them, but if you like a more abundant arrangement you can fill in the gaps with small filler flowers like the spray Chrysanthemums. These can be sectionally cut as they have smaller stems coming off the main stem (see conditioning and care on page 32 for details on how to use multi-headed stems) to allow the flowers to be used throughout the arrangement.

Step 7

Admire your work by placing it somewhere you can see it all the time for maximum pleasure.

VARIATIONS

Gather some flowers from your garden and make a beautiful garden-style arrangement.

Make an all-foliage bowl arrangement.

You can make a bowl arrangement when a few of your flowers have died off, or just remove a few from the vase to make another display for your home – let your creativity run wild. I quite like having this display on the mantlepiece in my front room or sitting on my kitchen table. The ingredients are the maximum amount needed for a bowl of this size.

Bud vase arrangement

In an ideal world I would have flowers in every room 365 days of the year, but the reality is flowers are a luxury item. This book is all about getting the most out of every last bloom, and a lovely way to enjoy the last surviving flowers from a bouquet is by placing them in bud vases.

A bud vase will typically hold a few flowers, but they can also be used to exhibit a single magnificent and eye-catching stem, or even aromatic flowers like garden Roses snipped straight from the bush. They come in all shapes, sizes and colours and are hugely popular dotted down a table in varying heights for an informal dinner party or wedding.

From our original vase arrangement there will be a few last longing blooms like Lisianthus, Alstroemeria and Carnations that may have outlasted the others, so here I will show you how a few blooms in bud vases strategically placed around your home can improve your mood, enhance interiors and bring real joy.

FLOWERS AND FOLIAGE

whatever flowers you may have left from your vase or bowl arrangement

OTHER ITEMS

a few bud vases

florists' scissors

Project 01

Informal table arrangement

Step 1

Fill the clean bud vases with water and make sure the flower stems have been recut.

Step 2

Place a few focal, filler and line flowers in the bud vases, cutting the stems so the heights are varied.

Step 3

Place the bud vases informally down the middle of your table, or group a few together for a more impactful table arrangement.

Project 02

Mantle arrangement

Follow the same process as for an informal table arrangement, and place your bud vases in groups or dotted across the mantle for a gorgeous splash of floral joy.

If you don't want to formally arrange your bud vases, you could dot them around your home. What could be nicer than looking at an individual Rose while you are cooking or washing up in the kitchen – or try placing a vase on your bedside table: waking up to the sight of flowers will certainly set you up for the day ahead.

Minimalist arrangement

Sometimes less is more. Looking at the beauty and arranging just a few flower stems can bring immense joy and pleasure. This style of arrangement is similar to the Japanese tradition of flower arranging called Ikebana. Ikebana is a classical art and is steeped in history; it's based on a harmony of simple linear construction and appreciation of the subtle beauty of flowers. With this wonderful practice come a lot of rules and meaning, and it can take many years of training to fully understand what each flower placement and plant material signifies. Whilst I do not profess to be an Ikebana specialist, I do love this minimal style and there are many modern takes on it. Here I will show you my version of this wonderful style, using just a few flowers so the real beauty of each one can be fully appreciated.

FLOWERS AND FOLIAGE

8 Gerberas

OTHER ITEMS

oasis fix adhesive tack

pin frog or kenzan around 6.5 cm (2½ in) in diameter

small bowl around 10 cm (4 in) in diameter

florists' scissors or secateurs

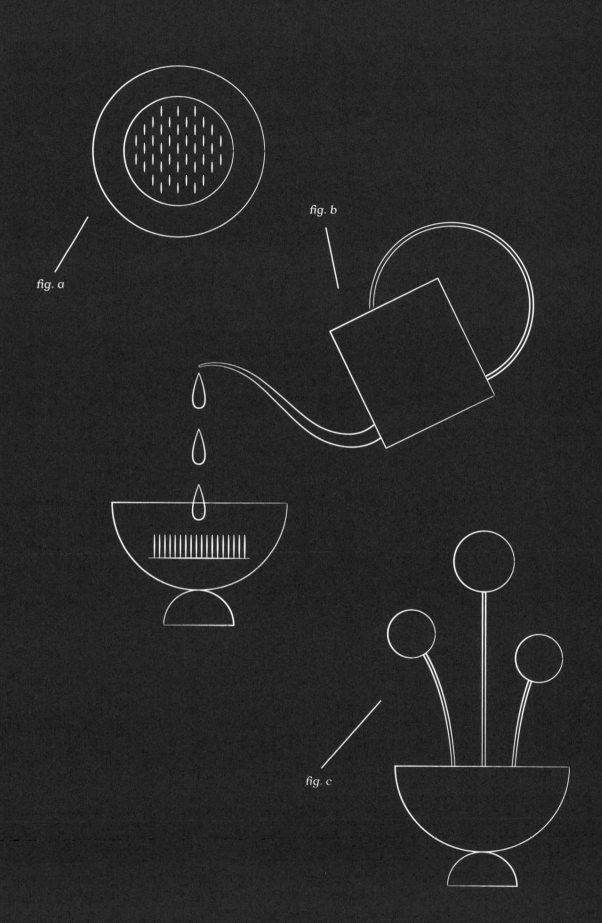

fig. a

fig. b

fig. c

Step 1

Pull a short length of adhesive tack and peel off the paper backing.

Step 2

Stick the adhesive tack around the edge of your pin frog or kenzan, making sure some of it slightly overlaps the edge *(see fig. a, opposite)*.

Step 3

Stick your pin frog or kenzan into your dry, clean bowl and then fill the bowl with water *(see fig. b, opposite)*.

Step 4

Condition the Gerberas as explained on page 32. Cut two to around the same length as the diameter of your bowl and place them facing towards you, slightly spaced apart at a slight angle.

Step 5

Continue to build up your arrangement by cutting your stems slightly longer each time to form a bit of a diamond shape. The idea of the arrangement is to see the flowers, allowing space between them, and to create lines (see fig. c, opposite).

TIPS AND TRICKS

Use your creativity to make your flower placements – this style of arrangement allows you to create amazing shapes using minimal design.

VARIATION

I have used one type of flower to show how to create lines and shapes, but you can mix up the arrangement with different flowers and foliage – just keep the number of stems to a minimum. Many Ikebana-style arrangements only use around five stems and some use only one – this could be a single cherry blossom branch placed in your pin frog. What a treat. Once you start exploring this wonderful flower practice you will discover the true beauty of individual flowers: fuss-free, elegant and beautiful.

LIFE CYCLE OF A TULIP

DAY 1

At this stage, Tulips should be upright and standing to attention, giving a gorgeous display in your favourite vase. If the stems are a bit floppy, cut them at an angle, remove some of the leaves, and revive them as explained on page 35. Remove the paper and replace the tulips in a vase of clean water and enjoy.

DAY 5

Tulips continue to grow even as a cut flower, so the length of the stems will continue to evolve, twist and bend. They are really versatile and the shape can easily be changed to make them look like an open flower by reflexing – see page 97.

Tulips

Tulips are a wonderful spring flower and the shape and form can be changed with interesting and evocative results. They can be tricky customers to look after, but there are some simple tips to get the most out of these amazing and sometimes overlooked blooms.

Tulips are a very easy flower to grow, so why not have a go at popping some bulbs in the ground and waiting for the magic to happen. If you don't have a garden you can grow tulips in a container or large pot. Tulips can be grown inside, but make sure you buy indoor varieties.

Try growing different varieties: my favourites are parrot and double varieties.

Mix and match reflexed tulips with ones that have been left natural. Simply arrange them in a flower frog and put the finished arrangement in a place where their beauty can be fully appreciated.

DAY 10

This is the stage when I love Tulips the most – they are so wonderful flopping over the side of a vase in a cascade, fully bloomed, looking truly delicious. This is a sight to behold, so never be tempted to throw them away before you get the chance to enjoy them just before the end of their life.

FLOWERS

TO   GIVE

All florists love to give and make bouquets as gifts, and I am no different. Bouquets bring that immediate rush of joy, and the recipient then enjoys a wonderful few days of colour and beauty. Bouquets are for a moment of celebration, to mark a special occasion or to just put a smile on someone's face.

The first project in this section looks at how you can create a beautiful and interesting hand-tied bouquet, using flowers that are readily available. Then I show you how using one type of flower grouped together looks amazing and makes a wonderful gift for a friend – or one that you may be tempted to keep all for yourself. And for something that will last a little longer, try the final project in which we will pot up an Orchid.

Structural hand-tied bouquet

Like any florist, I am drawn to the most beautiful abundant blooms each season can offer, but what if you aren't a florist and you cannot access these blooms? How can you still create a beautiful, interesting, different hand-tied bouquet? The answer is to keep it simple and use what is accessible to you.

This bouquet really concentrates on grouping the different flower types together, allowing you to enjoy the forms and shapes of flowers without the use of much foliage. Don't be put off by the misconceptions of others who deem some of these flowers unpopular. When using this combination of unexpected and readily available flowers, prepare to be surprised. You can vary the number of flowers used dependant on what size bouquet you wish to make. The ingredients below will make a medium-sized bouquet.

FLOWERS AND FOLIAGE

5 Lilies

6 stems of foliage or twigs from your garden, foraged or purchased from your local florist

10 Roses

5 Carnations

5 Alstroemeria

5 Gerberas

OTHER ITEMS

florists' scissors or secateurs

string

gift wrapping material such as tissue paper, newspaper or brown paper

Sellotape (Scotch tape)

Step 1

Condition the flowers as described on page 32. Take extra care when removing thorns from Roses – I find using a knife the best tool to do this.

Step 2

Start by taking two of the Lilies and a few stems of foliage in your left hand (if you are right-handed, and vice versa if you are left-handed). Place three of the Roses to the left of the Lilies at an angle of around 25 degrees, then place two of the Carnations just to the left of that until you have a fan of seven stems plus foliage.

Step 3

With all hand-tied bouquets the goal is to achieve a spiral of stems, which allows the bouquet to sit nicely in a vase. When the stems are cut this technique also means they will not break. To achieve this, start to turn the seven stems by taking them into your other hand and twisting them about a half turn.

Step 4

Put the bouquet back in your original hand, add in three Alstroemeria and two more Roses in exactly the same manner and then twist again. You can vary the height of the stems you are adding for interest and to allow each flower to be seen when placed in a vase.

VARIATIONS

Make this bouquet using all the different coloured flowers for a more vibrant look.

Use more foliage from the garden or foraged foliage to make a wild natural-looking bouquet.

Gift wrap using only one piece of paper to allow more of the arrangement to be seen.

Give the bouquet in an inexpensive vase, saving time on wrapping and allowing the stems to drink all the time as they are already in water.

Step 5

Keep adding in the groupings of flowers until all the flower material has been used, finishing with a few stems of foliage and a final Lily.

Step 6

Holding the bouquet in your left hand, tie it by wrapping the string around the stems several times with your right hand and then tie just under the lowest flower head point – this is called the binding point. Once you have secured the bouquet loosely, place it on your table and then secure it more tightly, finishing with a knot. Try not to tie the arrangement too tightly or you risk the danger of breaking any delicate stems.

Step 7

Cut off the ends of the flower stems until they are all level. Make sure they are cut at a slight angle to maximise the cut surface area, which helps with the take-up of water. Keep the stem length quite long because this allows the recipient to trim them down to the height of their vase, and will allow them to be recut every few days when the water is changed. This will keep the flowers looking at their best for longer.

Step 8

If you want to gift wrap, lay the bouquet on your table and choose two sheets of gift wrap. Fold one piece of paper to make two triangles that are slightly off kilter to form two points, then place the flowers on one piece and tape into place. Reverse this with the other piece to ensure the bouquet is fully wrapped.

Step 9

If you are travelling with the bouquet, place it in a bucket of water for transfer – or if this is not possible, wrap the stems in damp kitchen towel and remove before delivery.

One-flower type arrangement

Instead of looking at different flowers to combine, why not just give one type? There are so many opportunities with single-flower arrangements: they can look stylish; sophisticated and chic; or gathered and natural. There is nothing more pleasing to the eye than a mass of Carnations, clouds of Hydrangeas, or beautiful freshly cut Dahlias from your garden, wrapped in newspaper or anything you can get your hands on. By using one flower type you can combine myriad of different colours, go for one colour, or use different gradients of one colour. The opportunities are endless and really exciting – there is so much for you to explore.

FLOWERS AND FOLIAGE

> choose one flower type; here I am using Hydrangeas

OTHER ITEMS

> florists' scissors or secateurs
>
> string, ribbon or net
>
> gift wrapping material like tissue paper, newspaper or brown paper
>
> Sellotape (Scotch tape)
>
> scissors

Step 1

Condition the flowers as explained on page 32, stripping all the leaves from the stems working from the top to the bottom. With Hydrangeas you can choose to leave some of the lovely large leaves on or remove them all.

Step 2

Loosely lay the flowers on the table in groups on top of each other for an informal look, or if you would like a round bouquet follow the technique for a structured hand-tied bouquet on pages 64–67.

Step 3

Cut off the ends of the flower stems until they are all level. Make sure they are cut at a slight angle to maximise the cut surface area, which helps with the take-up of water. Keep the stem length quite long as this allows the recipient to trim them down to the height of their vase, and will allow them to be recut every few days when the water is changed. This will keep the flowers looking at their best for longer.

Step 4

Lay the bouquet on your table and choose two sheets of gift wrap. Fold one piece of paper to make two triangles that are slightly off kilter to form two points, place the flowers on one piece and tape into place. Reverse this with the other piece to ensure the bouquet is fully wrapped and tie with beautiful ribbon, string or something a bit different like net.

Step 5

If you are travelling with the bouquet, place it in a bucket of water for transfer – or if this is not possible, wrap the stems in damp kitchen towel and remove before delivery.

VARIATION

Try using different flowers to create this bouquet. Carnations, Sweet Peas, Stocks, Lilies or Irises work really well.

Potted orchid bowl

While bouquets are a wonderful gift, I often think about how I can give a floral gift that lasts a little longer. When I worked for a wonderful London florist I was tasked with potting up lots of beautiful Orchids into bowls and displaying them at varying heights and sizes to make amazing stand-out displays for the shop. These were not for sale, but I always thought they should be. If you want to give a gift that lasts a bit longer than a bouquet, then a potted bowl of exotic Orchids is a great choice. Orchids are readily accessible in supermarkets and most garden/DIY centres. They come in miniature and full-size forms. Massed together in a simple ceramic bowl they will give months of pleasure.

FLOWERS AND FOLIAGE

3–5 Orchid plants in pots

OTHER ITEMS

large ceramic or metal bowl, slightly deeper than the potted Orchid plants

plastic sheet

scissors

stones for drainage

compost

stones or moss for decoration

Step 1

Line your bowl with plastic – I use a bin liner to give an extra protective layer, Then spread a thin layer of stones on the bottom for drainage.

Step 2

Place your Orchids in position, still in their plastic pots, in the areas you wish them to sit – they can be grouped together in the middle or spaced apart.

Step 3

Fill in the gaps between your Orchids with compost until the plastic pots can no longer be seen.

Step 4

Cover the compost with decorative stones or moss to finish.

Orchids are readily available and long lasting.

Water the orchids about every 15 days, making sure not to overwater.

The orchid bloom should last around three months and these flowers do enjoy being in a sunny spot in your home.

Orchids also like humidity, so every once in a while take your arrangement into the bathroom while taking a hot shower.

VARIATIONS

For a seasonal arrangement try using spring bulbs or butterfly-like Cyclamen.

For a plant-loving friend try making up a bowl of ferns and succulents and any other long-lasting accessible plant. The choice and list of variations are endless and I hope you have lots of fun trying out different mixtures.

LIFE CYCLE OF A CORAL CHARM PEONY

DAY 1

The Coral Charm Peony arrives as a tight pink ball. At this stage the real beauty cannot be appreciated fully, but I do love them at this stage bundled together in a vase, looking like a gorgeous bunch of pink tennis balls. The anticipation of what is to come makes this stage very bearable.

DAYS 1–3

Depending on the weather and the age of the flower when purchased, the petals will start to open. If it is particularly warm weather the flower can be in full bloom in a few hours – how amazing is that?

DAYS 4–5

Your Peonies will now be at their absolute best. On occasion there are some that may take a few days longer to open, but on average this is the length of time it normally takes for them to bloom. You will now see where they get their name of Coral Charm from, as the petals slowly transition from pink to the amazing coral colour they are so well renowned for.

74

Coral Charm Peony

What is it about the Peony that everyone loves? Is it the fact that it is only around for a very short time each year, making it really special? Is it the multiple petals that start off looking like a scoop of ice cream, then explode into a multiple array of petal upon petal? I struggle to find a person who doesn't love a Peony. One of my favourites and most available in supermarkets is the Sarah Bernhardt variety, but the one that is so incredible is the Coral Charm Peony. Starting off as the ugly duckling but blossoming into a beautiful swan, the transition of this gorgeous bloom is nothing short of incredible.

DAYS 6–8 As with most incredibly special flowers like these their shelf life isn't the longest, and sometimes they will fade away around Day 5 – especially in warm conditions. The older these flowers get, the more faded the petals become. I often wonder at how amazing nature is; starting life as a very pink flower and ending up nearly blond in colour is something that I never get bored with looking at. The only downside is at this stage they sometimes give off a bit of a strange smell, but I for one am willing to put up with this. I encourage you not to throw them away until the now transparent petals slowly start to drop. They are truly the most delicious blooms.

FLOWERS

TO

WEAR

I love making flowers to wear – there is something really special about wearing flowers, because it normally happens on special, happy, joyous occasions. Personally, I see nothing wrong with wearing flowers every day – but I would say that being a florist. Wiring flowers can be both frustrating and satisfying in equal amounts, but once you have practised it is something you will love doing. Having this skill is very useful, especially if you wish to do wedding work. I have given some details on how to wire flowers on pages 24–25.

In this section I show you how to make a corsage with fresh flowers, and then a flower crown, a delicate wrist corsage/bracelet and a hair comb, all using dried flowers. The last three can be made by buying one large bunch of dried flowers, which are available to purchase online. Make sure when buying your mixed bunch you choose one that has lots of small-headed dried flowers, such as Broom and Limonium, plus a few larger flowers, such as Straw Flowers, so you have lots of choice and variation.

Fresh flower corsage

One of the first wired pieces I made when I was training to be a florist was a wired corsage.

The reason this is taught first is because you don't have to wire too many materials, and if you are going to do wedding work it is a really lovely, popular piece for ladies to wear when part of the bridal party. I like to make corsages more like a buttonhole rather than in the traditional style, which is double ended. By using only a few materials you can make something lightweight, gorgeous and stylish.

FLOWERS AND FOLIAGE

a choice of:

2 stems spray Rose

A few dried flowers for texture

A few leaves of choice

OTHER ITEMS

florists' scissors or secateurs

thin floristry wires, around 26-gauge

wire cutters

florists' stem tape

thin satin or silk ribbon

ribbon-cutting scissors

corsage pin

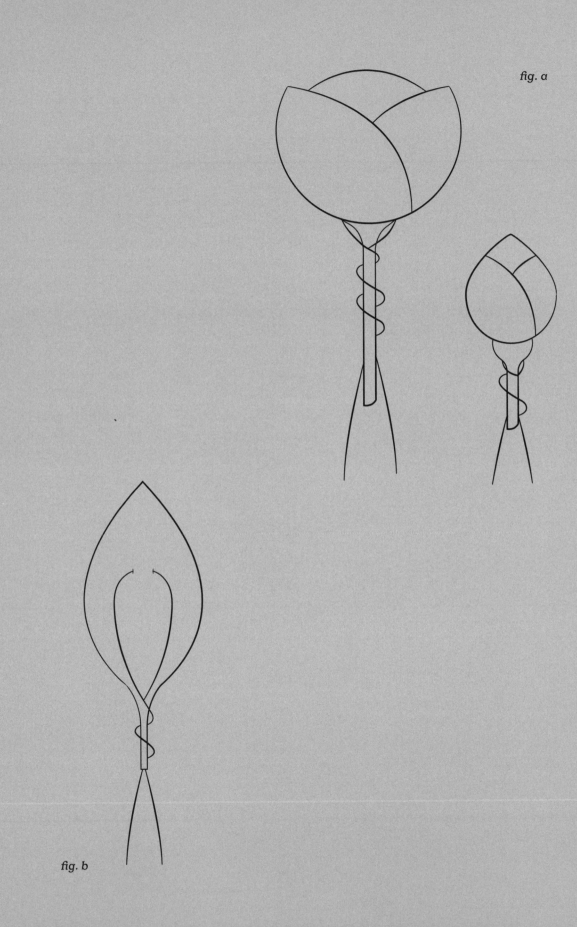

fig. a

fig. b

Step 1

Cut two spray Roses, a few buds if there are some available on the spray Rose stems and a few leaves, leaving around 1–2 cm (⅜–¾ in) of stem to allow easy wiring.

Step 2

Wire all the flowers and leaves as per instructions on pages 24–25 (see also fig. a and b, opposite).

Step 3

Use one of your wired leaves to form a support and backing for the flowers. Then play around with the configuration of your wired flowers – it's always best to start with one of your larger blooms and then add in the small blooms or buds around it.

Step 4

Once you are happy with the placement, secure the blooms using stem tape by binding all the wires together. You should end up with around 4 cm (1½ in) of wire left once you have taped your corsage together – if it is longer than that, cut the wires to around that length.

Step 5

Finish your corsage by wrapping thin ribbon around the taped wires and add a pin to allow attachment.

Dried flower crown

Dried flowers have seen a massive revival of late. People like to see the beauty in flowers that have gone through their lifecycle and are still able to offer a faded beauty of their former selves. I have to admit I have never really been a huge fan of making dried flower bouquets, but that got me thinking about how else they can be used, and wearable flowers is where I think they come into their own. I like the idea of using dried flowers to wear because you don't have the worry about them dying or wilting. Flower crowns are one of the most popular wearable flowers to make – they can reflect different moods and be styled for different occasions. With the wide range of dried flowers available you could make a really colourful crown for a festival, for a bride-to-be on her hen party, or you could make a natural, subtle crown for a bride to wear on her wedding day.

FLOWERS AND FOLIAGE

around 35 stems of dried flowers from your mixed bunch

OTHER ITEMS

thick aluminium or green florists' wires

wire cutters

florists' stem tape – I prefer the paper sticky type to the waterproof type, but either are fine

scissors

reel wire

silk or satin ribbons

Step 1

Wrap a length of the aluminium wire three quarters around your head to make the shape of the crown and then cut the wire. Bend back one loop at each end for the ribbons to go through. Cover the wire with florists' tape by twisting and stretching it along your wire. This provides some grip when attaching your dried flowers (see fig. a, opposite).

Step 2

Cut small bunches of your dried flowers and lay them in piles. I like to group the same flower types together so I can use some from each pile as I am going along – this makes it really easy to make sure your crown has variation.

Step 3

Place a couple of dried flowers from your pile on top of the taped wire and bind them on by winding the reel wire around the end of the bunch a number of times (see fig. b, opposite). When wrapping the wires try not to do it too tightly because you want the flowers to be able to move a little when you are wearing your crown.

Step 4

Continue to add in the flowers, mixing them up from your separate piles, slightly layering and overlapping them over your previous attached flower stems. This crown is very delicate and subtle – if you wanted to make a bolder, bigger crown you could use larger and bigger groupings of flowers.

Step 5

Once you have completely covered the base wire with flowers, wrap the wire tightly over the last stems and cut off any overhanging stems. I like to make sure that I have a larger flower at each end so that the ribbon loops are covered.

Step 6

Finish your crown by threading your ribbon though the loops, tie in a bow to the size of your head and enjoy.

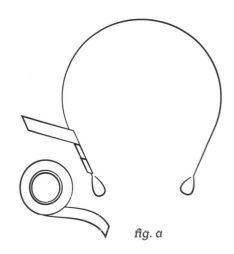

fig. a

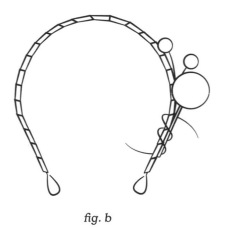

fig. b

VARIATIONS

This crown can be made with fresh flowers. The main difference is that the flowers will need to be wired and taped individually to make sure that they last out of water. See pages 24–25 on how to wire a flower. I love making one-flower type crowns and find that a good flower to practise with is Sweet William, which can be readily purchased in spring time. Their sturdy multiheaded blooms make them the perfect material to practise your wiring techniques.

If you didn't want to make this on an aluminium wire you can use the same technique on an Alice band. I find Alice bands a good choice for children as they tend to stay on the head much better.

I like to make flower crowns about three-quarters the size of the head. This is for two reasons: full crowns never seem to fit the head perfectly even if you have measured exactly, and a crown that is three-quarters of the head size allows you to add in ribbon, which can be tied beautifully. Flowing ribbons at the back of the crown are a lovely addition, especially if they are being made for tiny bridesmaids or a festival bride.

Wrist corsage

The mention of a wrist corsage might conjure up thoughts of huge silk blooms with large ribbons adorning the wrist, similar to those worn by girls to a prom. This need not be the case; a tasteful and simple wrist corsage like this one can be worn for many different occasions. It also offers a great alternative to a bridesmaid's bouquet, or for mums in the bridal party instead of a traditional corsage on their dresses. I have always found wrist corsages a little tricky to make, but using dried flowers instead of fresh gives much more flexibility because the flowers are a little easier to manipulate. Once you have perfected this technique there is nothing to stop you making a fresh flower wrist corsage – just remember to wire and tape your fresh flowers before construction (pages 24–25).

FLOWERS AND FOLIAGE

around 15 stems
of dried flowers
from your mixed bunch

OTHER ITEMS

florists' wire, around
24-gauge, or aluminium wire

wire cutters

florists' stem tape

scissors

reel wire

silk or satin ribbon

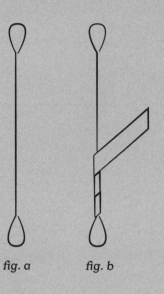

fig. a   fig. b

fig. e

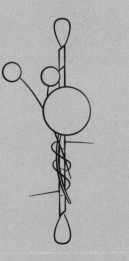

fig. c   fig. d

Step 1

For your base, cut two pieces of florists' wire, with one around 5 cm (2 in) longer than the other – measure it on your wrist for size. Wrap the two pieces together to make a firm support and then make one loop at each end with the longer piece of wire (see fig. a, opposite). If you are using aluminium wire you only need one length as it is a lot thicker; cut to size and follow the same instruction as for florists' wire.

Step 2

Wrap the florists' stem tape around the florists' or aluminium wire, making sure all the wire is covered (see fig. b, opposite). As the florists' tape is a little bit sticky this makes the dried flowers a bit easier to attach to the base.

Step 3

Lay a few flowers onto the top of the wire base and wrap your reel wire around the stems – once should be enough to secure them (see fig. c, opposite). Remember to mix and vary your flowers for interest.

Step 4

Continue to add in the flowers, slightly layering and overlapping them over your previous attached flower stems (see fig. d, opposite).

Step 5

Once you have covered the small wire base completely with flowers, wrap your wire round the end about three times and then cut the wire, making sure the end is tucked in so no sharp wires are exposed.

Step 6

Thread your ribbon through both loops, making sure that it goes from one end to the other (see fig. e, opposite). As you are threading the ribbon right the way though this will act a support for the wrist corsage and make it really comfortable for the wearer because the wire will be backed by the ribbon.

Dried flower comb

Now you have mastered the art of wiring you will have the confidence to work on smaller items. A flower comb is a really lovely way to wear flowers in your hair, and is also a simple accessory for children to wear – I find that children don't tend to fiddle with them as much as they do with a flower crown. A flower comb is a really versatile hair accessory and I make a lot of them for brides and their bridal party. Combs can be worn on various parts of the head in different styles; a really popular way is secured into a lovely low ponytail. One of the best things about a flower comb is the length of time it takes to make. Because you are binding flowers onto a much smaller base they are pretty quick to assemble, and again you don't have to worry about the flowers wilting as they are already dried.

FLOWERS AND FOLIAGE

around 10 stems
of dried flowers from
your mixed bunch

OTHER ITEMS

reel wire

plastic flower comb

wire cutters

scissors

Step 1

Place your chosen flowers in their individual flower types – I like to do this to make it easier to construct because you can take a few dried blooms from each bunch to create a varied design.

Step 2

Attach your reel wire to one end of the hair comb, winding it through the teeth a few times so it is fully secure (see fig. a, oppposite).

Step 3

Starting with a few flowers, lay them on top of the hair comb and wrap your wire around the stems. At this point you need to think about the size and shape of the comb, plus where it will sit on your head. If the comb is for a child, you wouldn't want the materials to be very big as the comb would look out of proportion with their head.

Step 4

Continue to add in the flowers, mixing them up from your separate piles, slightly layering and overlapping them over your previous attached flower stems. Each time you wind the wire round your next stems it must pass through the teeth of the comb (see fig. b, opposite). It is nice to mix up textures and you could even introduce other materials like netting or some fresh foliage that will dry in time. Mixing and matching materials adds interest and allows you to experiment.

Step 5

Once you have reached the end of your comb you can reverse the last few materials so both ends of the comb look the same. This can be really tricky when you are learning how to make a flower comb – the best way is to take a few stems and lay them under the existing flowers at the end of your comb, binding tightly with your reel wire. Alternatively, you can just finish the comb by placing a slightly larger bloom at the end to nicely cover the wires.

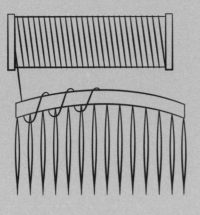

fig. a

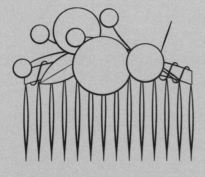

fig. b

VARIATION

Now you are a master at wiring, another nice way to wear flowers in your hair is to individually wire a few blooms and thread them through your hair. To achieve this, take a few dried flowers and wrap your reel wire round the bottom of the stems. Then take a length of green florists' wire and cut to the desired length. Using your florists' stem tape (I like to use the paper type), attach your bunch to the wire by wrapping the tape around the small bunch and down to the bottom of the green florists' wire. Insert into your hair and enjoy.

As with a flower crown you can make these as large or small as you like, and vary the materials you use to suit the occasion. It may be that sometimes you wear one just because!

I like to make delicate designs using small-headed dried flowers, but that is of course my preference. The best thing about all of this is that you should have plenty of flowers left from your dried bunch to practise a few different designs.

FLOWERS

FOR

CELEBRATION

Celebrations can be large or small, intimate or elaborate. Whatever occasion it may be, flowers will always add something special. There are so many different types of arrangements that can be made for a celebration, but I have concentrated on three that will work in different settings, offering maximum versatility: a large urn, a long low table decoration and garlands.

My large urn arrangement is very abundant, and celebrates seasonal early summer flowers, but this and all the other arrangements in this section can be made at any time of the year using flowers you have available. Repurposing flowers is one of my favourite things to do; it allows me to practise my technique, try different things and ensures I get the most out of my flowers. The long and low table decoration reuses flowers from the large urn. It is lovely for guests to be able to take a few blooms and enjoy them in their homes, arranging them in different ways.

I have included garlands in flowers for a celebration because they are hugely versatile and can be used in so many settings and not just for Christmas. You could make a simple garland for an informal gathering, on a mantle or to decorate stairs in the home. You may want to wind them round pillars or use them to decorate chairs along the aisle at a wedding. The opportunities are endless and I love the way that they can wind down a table, snaking in and out of cutlery, glasses and candles.

Stand-out urn arrangement

I love making a large urn arrangement. I think it is often much nicer to make one stand-out arrangement than lots of little ones; an arrangement that makes people stop in their tracks and take notice. This style of arrangement can be made for any type of celebration – a garden party, a wedding or an elaborate dinner party. Early summer has some of the nicest flowers on offer and it means that really abundant arrangements can be made without huge cost. I have listed the maximum number of flowers you should need for this arrangement, which will vary depending on the size of the urn. I have chosen the forever-loved Peony as my focal flower and teamed it with Roses and other garden-style flowers for a lush, green, natural look. Peonies will always be the most requested flower by brides and flower-lovers alike. As their season is short I make sure that I use them at every opportunity, and I am so happy to see them on sale in some supermarkets so these treasured flowers can be enjoyed by more of us, not just those who have access to the flower market. Other focal flowers that will work well in this arrangement are Sunflowers and fully open Oriental Lilies.

FLOWERS AND FOLIAGE

20 stems of foliage cut from your garden, foraged or purchased from your local florist

10 Stocks, Delphiniums or Snapdragons

10 Peonies

10 Roses

10 Gerberas

10 Lisianthus

10 spray Chrysanthemums

5 Carnations

OTHER ITEMS

urn, a wide-necked urn or a more traditional Victorian-type urn

plastic container to place in your urn if it has a drainage hole

chicken wire

wire cutters

florists' pot tape

florists' scissors, secateurs and knife

Step 1

Prepare the urn with the chicken wire as explained on page 22. Condition the flowers as explained on page 32. Take extra care when removing thorns from Roses – I find using a knife the best tool to do this.

Step 2

Green up your arrangement by placing the foliage in the chicken wire frame, spaced out and in a loose style. Make sure you have some foliage around the base of the urn, a high point and a low point to create an asymmetrical shape that works wonderfully when using urns. Next add in a few line flowers (Delphiniums, Stocks or Snapdragons).

Step 3

Now place some focal flowers (Peonies/Roses) and a few more line flowers (Delphiniums, Stocks or Snapdragons) mirroring your foliage, keeping a few taller than the others. They can also be grouped together or spaced throughout the arrangement at varying heights on both sides of the urn. Don't cut your stems too short in the first instance – it is always better to reduce the stem length gradually because once you've made that cut it is final. I like to group a few flowers together at the base of the vase to make a focal point.

Step 4

We are now about halfway though the arrangement. At this point have a look at your urn from a distance and check that you are happy with the shape. Make sure that you dig a few blooms in deep so they are only barely seen. This will give depth and volume and will make sure that the final arrangement looks three dimensional and not flat.

Step 5

Continue adding in your focal Peonies and Roses and your Gerberas and Lisianthus by following the same process as in step three. Stand away from your arrangement from time to time to check your flower placement. Keep placing the flowers and varying the depth and height. This is a celebration of flowers so the final arrangement will be very flower heavy, with blooms close to each other to create a very luxurious look.

Step 6

When you have placed all your flowers, add in the spray Chrysanthemums and Carnations to fill in all the gaps the arrangement.

Step 7

Make a final check from both sides of the arrangement to make sure you are happy with the positioning of your flowers. As this is supported by chicken wire it allows you to move the flowers until you are completely satisfied, but don't over-think it – creativity comes from the heart and sometimes too much fiddling doesn't always improve the arrangement.

On page 19 I have detailed when the most beautiful flowers are in season, so if you fancy making an arrangement with a seasonal twist you will know when they can be purchased.

If this arrangement is likely to be placed against a wall and not viewed from every point, you can put fewer flowers at the back of the arrangement and more of your material at the front. If it is going to viewed from all angles make sure your material is spaced out between the back and front of the arrangement.

Long and low floral arrangement for a table

One of the first things I learned to make was a long low table arrangement. When I trained as florist we made these in a traditional way using floral foam, which is not very environmentally friendly as it doesn't decompose. I have brought this arrangement right up to date, using sustainable techniques that you can use in any size or shape vessel. I have reused the flowers from the large urn as an arrangement of that size is always a bit too big for one person to take home – here is a lovely way to enjoy the beautiful booms for a while longer, and it would look great in the middle of a table while having a lovely informal meal with friends.

FLOWERS AND FOLIAGE

10 stems of foliage cut from your garden, foraged or purchased from your local florist

5 Stocks, Delphiniums or Snapdragons

3–5 Peonies

5 Roses

5 Gerbera

5 Lisianthus

5 spray Chrysanthemums

5 Carnations

OTHER ITEMS

long low trough-style vase around 28 cm (11 in) long, 10 cm (4 in) deep, 9 cm (3½ in) high

chicken wire

wire cutters

florists' pot tape

florists' scissors or secateurs

Step 1

Prepare the vase with the chicken wire as explained on page 22. Condition the flowers as explained on page 32.

Step 2

Green up your arrangement by placing the foliage in the chicken wire frame, spaced out and in a loose style. Make sure you have some foliage around the base of the vase and some at higher points spread right across the container.

Step 3

Add in your line flowers (Delphinium, Stocks or Snapdragons) mirroring your foliage, and keeping a few taller that the others. These can also be grouped together or spaced throughout the arrangement.

Step 4

Start placing your focal flowers (Peonies and Roses) at varying heights on both sides of the vase. Don't cut your stems too short in the first instance; it is always better to reduce the stem length gradually – once you've made that cut it is final. I like to group a few flowers together at the base of the vase to make a focal point.

Step 5

At this point have a look at your vase from a distance and check that you are happy with the shape. Do make sure that you dig a few blooms deep in the arrangement. This will give the final arrangement depth and volume.

Step 6

Continue adding in the Roses, Gerberas and Lisianthus by following the same process as in step three. Pay attention to the height, spacing out the flowers and varying the depth of the flowers. With this style of arrangement, I like the faces of the flowers to be seen in full so make sure that when you place your flowers the beauty of them can be fully appreciated.

Step 7

When you have placed all your flowers, add in the spray Chrysanthemums and Carnations.

Step 8

Make a final check from both sides of the arrangement to make sure you are happy with the positioning of your flowers. As this is supported by chicken wire it allows you to move the flowers until you are completely satisfied, but don't over-think it – creativity comes from the heart and sometimes too much fiddling doesn't always improve the arrangement.

Step 9

Place your finished arrangement in the middle of the table for you and your guests to admire while enjoying a wonderful meal.

VARIATIONS

This arrangement will work in different settings. Why not place it on a mantlepiece for an abundant addition to your living space.

As the vessel is low and long, after your meal you can place it on a windowsill, or on your favourite cabinet or sideboard.

As this arrangement is for a table you do not want to make it higher than around 20 cm (8 in) so people can see over the arrangement. You will be able to have a few higher flowers, but make sure these are spaced out so views aren't obstructed.

Garlands

I wanted to dedicate a section of this book to garlands because many people over the years have asked me how to make one. This simple practice is sometimes a bit baffling for people, and there are many different ways of making a garland, which often confuses matters. Here are a couple of tried and tested methods that work well. I have started to experiment with incorporating different materials into my garlands such as rope, netting and ribbon for an interesting effect, which you could also try. The addition of texture brings a different dimension and can be tailored to the occasion you are making the garland for. I hope this will show you that you can make a garland out of most materials, so have fun, experiment and let your creativity run wild.

FLOWERS AND FOLIAGE

3 Peonies

3–5 Roses

3–5 Carnations

5 Lisianthus

5 Stocks, Delphiniums or Snapdragons

5 spray Chrysanthemums

20 stems of foliage either cut from your garden, foraged or purchased from your local florist, Ivy works especially well for garlands and other bushy foliage like Viburnum

OTHER ITEMS

florists' scissors or secateurs

washing line or thick string the length of garland you wish to make

reel wire, twine or thick string to bind the garland

20 floral water tubes

Project 01

Abundant floral table garland

For the first project we will use some of the flowers from the long and low arrangement on page 102 to make an abundant floral garland bound onto a washing line or string. This technique would allow for easy transportation, and the garlands could be wound around objects like pillars more easily.

Step 1

Condition the flowers as explained on page 32, and if you are reusing from a previous arrangement make sure all stems are given a fresh diagonal cut.

Step 2

Cut your washing line or string to the required length of the finished garland.

Step 3

Use the end of the reel wire or twine to bind three stems of your foliage to one end of the washing line/string.

Step 4

Continue to bind flowers and foliage in small bunches to the washing line/string. It is important that you position each new bunch just beneath the last addition to conceal any stalks.

Step 5

As you add more flowers and foliage make sure that you tightly bind the new piece to the last stem, so that the joined stems form a good sturdy extended backbone to the garland.

Step 6

When you have reached the end of the washing line/string, reverse the flowers and add in more small bunches to conceal the end of the stems. If you find this too tricky just continue adding in your bunches and flowers in the same direction until you reach the end of your garland.

Step 7

Lay the garland where you wish it to be positioned. It is important to cover any surfaces that may be damaged by moisture from the garland with a bit of cling film (plastic wrap). If you are hanging a garland around a doorway or pillar, make sure that you have nails or screws in place – but if it's in someone else's home or venue always ask permission before you start hammering nails into their walls.

Step 9

Make a final check that you are happy with your flower placements, adding any spare foliage to fill in the gaps.

Step 8

Now the garland is in place, you can add in your other flowers. Some flowers don't survive well without a water source, so you can place these in water tubes so they can still drink. First, fill your water tubes about two-thirds full. Next, cut the stems to the desired length and place in the water tubes. Now, thread and place the flowers into position in your garland, varying heights and depths.

TIPS AND TRICKS

The material listed on page 112 will make a garland of around 1 metre (39 in) long.

When you are initially starting to make garlands, it is sometimes easier to make small bundles of flowers first and secure them with string or reel wire. You can then attach them to your washing line or string with a bit more ease.

There are some flowers that will last much better without a water source. The flowers I would bind into the main garland would be the Lisianthus and spray Chrysanthemums. (See page 36 for more flowers that last well out of water.)

Project 02

Hydrangea garland

Hydrangeas will last a few hours out of water and as they have beautiful large heads of multiple flowers they make a wonderful flower for a garland. In this example there is no need to bind the garland onto a washing line or string, and this technique can be used if you are making garland that will lay flat all the time. Once you have finished with the garland, hydrangeas dry wonderfully and can be used in different projects or you could make a dried hydrangea garland in the Autumn combined with dried leaves. See page 118 for tips on drying these flowers and other uses.

FLOWERS AND FOLIAGE

6 Hydrangea heads

30 stems of mixed foliage (bushy style foliage like Ivy and Viburnum will work well again)

OTHER ITEMS

florists' scissors or secateurs

reel wire or string to bind your garland

Step 1

Condition your flowers as explained on page 32, leaving a few of the Hydrangea leaves on as they are large and form part of the foliage in your garland.

Step 2

Make six bundles of one Hydrangea and five stems of foliage, keeping the stems around 25 cm (10 in) long to start off with.

Step 3

Bind your bundles together by positioning each new bundle just beneath the last addition to conceal any stalks, and cut off any excess stems.

Step 4

Add in any spare foliage you may have to make a neat finish at the end of your garland.

Project 03

Berried ivy seasonal garland

Ivy can be found everywhere and the berried variety is one of my favourites. It looks amazing bundled together to make a beautiful garland for a simple but effective Christmas look. I generally forage berried ivy, and quite often I find it growing against fences, by railway lines and under railway bridges. If the bush is attached to someone's home, please ask permission before you take your scissors to it. Most times the owner will be happy for you to snip away – just make sure you do this sensitively so the bush doesn't look like it's been hacked and completely damaged.

Follow the instructions from Step 1 to Step 7 from the Abundant Floral Table Garland on pages 110–111, remembering to protect surfaces if you are going to hang this off a bannister or on a mantle.

VARIATIONS

Make a simple garland of pine branches to drape along a mantlepiece, made of two lengths of garland. You can try finishing this garland with rope and curtain tassels in the middle for interest.

Try laying blossom twigs and pieces of foliage down the middle of your table as a subtle nod to spring.

TIPS AND TRICKS

To make a 1-metre (39-in) long garland you will need around fifty stems of berried ivy to make it look lush and full, but you could use less for a thinner garland.

Scandi-style foraged wreath

I thought long and hard about featuring a wreath in this book, because access to the materials to make a traditional mossed Christmas wreath can be tricky. There are lots of florists, including myself, who offer wreath-making workshops where the materials are sourced for you, which makes this process much easier – but this does come at a price. With this in mind, I have decided to show you how to make a simple, low cost yet beautiful, Scandinavian-style minimal wreath using foraged materials. These wreaths won't last as long as a wreath made on a mossed base because there is nothing to provide moisture, but since the materials are foraged or cut from your garden there is nothing to stop you from refreshing it – or you could let nature take its course and allow it to dry beautifully.

FLOWERS AND FOLIAGE

around 20 pieces of mixed foliage – I used Ivy, Eucalyptus and foraged foliage from my garden

foliage that works well in this type of wreath are: berried and normal Ivy, Viburnum and Cypress Fir

OTHER ITEMS

florists' scissors or secateurs

metal craft ring in colour of your choice – I used a 12-cm (4¾-in) copper ring

reel wire

wire cutters

fig. a

fig. b

Step 1

Prepare your pieces of foliage, cutting the stems to around 10 cm (4 in) in length.

Step 2

Loop your reel wire round your ring around five times to make sure it is fully secure (see fig. a, opposite).

Step 3

Place a piece of your foliage and bind it onto the ring using the attached wire (see fig. b, opposite).

Step 4

Continue to bind on the materials, slightly overlapping each piece until around two-thirds of the ring is covered.

Step 5

Once all your material is bound onto the ring, cut your wire and tuck the end into the back of the foliage.

Step 6

Attach a new piece of wire to hang your wreath.

VARIATION

This style of wreath works really well with dried flowers and could be made at any time of the year, not just at Christmas.

THE BEAUTY OF THE HYDRANGEA

The Hydrangea fell out of favour for a while because they conjured up a picture of thatched cottages and twee villages, but I find them extremely useful – especially in wedding work. As they have enormous pompom heads of multiple flowers, they are excellent for filling up space in large arrangements. You would need around six Roses to take up the space of one Hydrangea in an arrangement, so they are a flower that should be considered when you need to cover large spaces. Arranged en-masse they also create a wonderful effect; I love that when they are grouped they look like a cloud of multiple-petalled loveliness.

I feel like this is the flower that keeps on giving, because they also dry beautifully. The ideal time to dry them is near the end of their season, which is late summer, especially if you are cutting them from a bush. The easiest method is to cut them as fresh flowers first and put them in a vase. As the days pass, allow the water to evaporate completely from the vase – this will normally take around two weeks maximum. At the end of this the Hydrangeas should feel dry to touch and ready to use as a dried flower. This versatile flower is a true star that should never be overlooked.

So how can you use them? I like to use them at Christmas as a welcome addition to my door wreath – you could also try making a whole wreath just of dried Hydrangeas. They can also be used in hanging arrangements as on page 126, or added to your fresh flower arrangements. If you cut off small pieces of the flower at the stalk, you could even try adding them into wearable flowers as on page 78. Hydrangeas can be tricky customers, especially in warm weather, and need to drink a lot. If your Hydrangea is looking a bit floppy, spray it since they drink really well through their petals. This particular flower also favours colder conditions before use.

Hydrangeas

Hydrangeas are described as cottage-style flowers that are easily grown in the garden or even in pots. Their huge heads of multiple flowers make this a bloom that cannot be ignored. One of the best things about growing Hydrangeas is that they return every year, often bigger than the previous year and offering so many opportunities. I love them because of the range of colours they come in: blue, white, pink and purple – and you sometimes see a beautiful transition in colour in just one bloom, which I find really fascinating.

LARGE

You will have to invest in a few materials for the projects in this section, but once you have them you can reuse them time and time again – this is the beauty of using sustainable floristry techniques.

Here you will find a floral arch, a lovely hanging Gypsophila cloud and a mantlepiece decoration, all using the same materials, allowing you to repurpose them to make the different arrangements.

ARRANGEMENTS

I was in two minds as to whether to include an arch in this book, but then I thought, why not – everyone loves an arch. Arches can be made and used in lots of different ways and settings, but they are mostly for large occasions. Most florists and flower arrangers alike love to create them, and they are a wonderful thing to assemble with a group, where like-minded people come together just to create. I used to scroll through social media and see amazing elaborate designs and wondered how on earth they are made – in this section you will find that the technique is so simple that you will make them just to practise using lots of cheap accessible flowers in different variations.

Hanging arrangements will need something to be suspended from, but you can easily tailor their shape to suit different locations so they can be very versatile. You can also make them larger or smaller – you just need to manipulate the chicken wire ball that forms the base.

Mantlepiece arrangements can be extremely versatile. Some mantlepieces are really grand and don't need too much decoration to elevate them, but normally they need serious floral attention – which is where the design in this section comes into its own.

Asymmetrical arch

Sometimes the hardest part of making a large floral arrangement is working out the mechanics and structure first, and I wanted to show you one of the easiest ways to make an asymmetrical arch. This type of arch is far more versatile than a traditional arch – you can tailor it to be a one-sided arrangement placed against a wall or an entrance, or make it much smaller to sit at the bottom of a staircase. It is most likely that you will make this arrangement for a more traditional setting, as a backdrop for a wedding or any other special occasion where people can be photographed in front of it. Here I have used Gypsophila, Carnations and Roses. Gypsophila and Carnations last incredibly well out of water so you can get away with only providing a water source for the Roses – and possibly for the Carnations if the arch is going to be up for a long time in a warm setting.

FLOWERS AND FOLIAGE

100 Gypsophila

50 Roses (largest ones you can afford)

50 Carnations

OTHER ITEMS

small bag of postcrete cement

2 small plastic buckets

2 copper pipes – one around 1.5 metre (59 in) and one around 1 metre (39 in) from a DIY store

roll of chicken wire

wire cutters

cable ties

florists' scissors, secateurs and knife

floral water tubes

Step 1

Prepare the structure – this is definitely easier with two people but can be managed by one. Start by mixing up your postcrete as per instructions on the packet. Place a copper pipe in the middle of each bucket and pour the postcrete around it – you only need enough to make the pole stand up, which should be a depth of around 12.5–15 cm (5–6 in). Hold the post until it is secure, the postcrete will stabilise quickly and should be set in around for 5–10 minutes. Once it is set, leave to firm up until the poles don't move. The great thing about this method is that the cement-filled buckets act as a weight, meaning that your finished arrangement will not topple over.

Step 2

Once the poles have set in the buckets, wrap a small amount of chicken wire around them and the buckets to create cylinders, securing them to the pole with cable ties. Attach some through the wire and around the copper poles for extra security. If you want the tops of the arrangement to curve in slightly, mould the chicken wire to this shape. Alternatively, you can follow the shape of the pole to make two parallel straight arrangements. The chicken wire provides the structure through which to thread the flowers and foliage.

Step 3

Condition the flowers as explained on page 32. Place your flowers in clean buckets of fresh water and place to one side.

Step 4

Start to cover the structure with Gypsophila which is your base material. Take around five to six stems at a time and feed them through the chicken wire. If you are finding any bunches hard to thread through, secure them with cable ties on the chicken wire structure.

Step 5

When you are happy and your wire is mostly covered, add in your Roses and Carnations. Place your Rose stems in water tubes as shown in step 8 on page 111, and then feed your flowers through the structure. These can be grouped, or you may prefer to space your flowers throughout the arch. Always vary the height and depth of your flowers so the arch doesn't look flat and one dimensional.

Step 6

Finish by filling in any gaps with spare Gypsophila stems.

This arch is best in terms of versatility and once you have practised the technique, you will have the confidence to try different materials, such as foliage and different flowers, to create beautiful stylish arches.

Hanging gypsophila flower cloud

So the arch has been made and the event is over, what do you do with the flowers? The answer is to make something new with the same flowers. The materials I used in the arch are long lasting, and the Gypsophila will dry out really nicely, giving you the option to make this arrangement when the stems are over a week old. Carnations and Roses will also last well over a week if they are looked after, so you don't have to repurpose your flowers straight away. This arrangement is light-hearted and can be used in many different settings. You can make lots of them to hang for a wedding reception or it could be made for a dinner party or baby shower. I hope you have lots of fun making this arrangement; starting on a small scale will allow you to perfect the technique. You can then have a go at making larger arrangements, using the same principles. As with every project in this book, I want to sow the seed by showing you the basics of a design, planting ideas on how to make them look a little bit different, and then hoping that you will experiment and make the design your own.

FLOWERS AND FOLIAGE

50 Gypsophila

30 Carnations

OTHER ITEMS

around 1 metre (39 in) square of chicken wire

wire cutters

15 cable ties

fishing wire 27 kg (60 lb) weight

scissors

Step 1

To prepare your structure, squash your chicken wire into a ball, making sure there are gaps to feed your flower material into. The ball will be around 30–40 cm (12–16 in) in diameter. Use several cable ties to secure the folded chicken wire to itself so that it does not spring open.

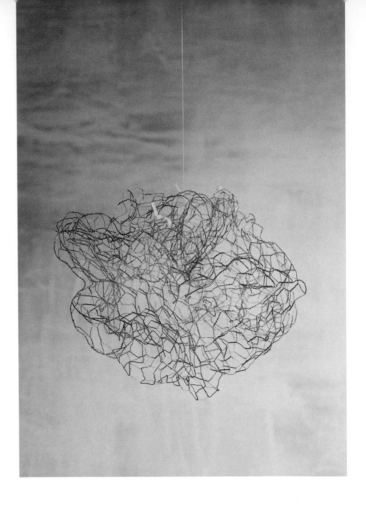

Step 2

Attach the fishing wire to the desired length and hang the structure at a height that is comfortable for you to work with it. I like to hang the structure from a ladder frame, or from the final point that I wish to suspend the ball from.

Step 3

Start to place your Gypsophila stems into the chicken wire structure making sure it is completely covered and is the desired shape. I haven't gone for formal ball look because I like it to look a bit cloud-like and a little more informal.

Step 4

Add in the Carnations, varying their depth and height for interest.

With hanging arrangements, you first need to establish where you can hang the finished item.

You can also tailor it into a different shape by manipulating the chicken wire. For instance, if you wanted to make a longer arrangement to hang over a table you could use a copper pipe as in in the arch example (page 124), wrapped in chicken wire attached with cable ties. You would then use the same technique as per this design to add the flowers and foliage.

Any material works in this design, and dried flowers look spectacular in a huge cloud – albeit costly if you have to purchase the dried materials.

I think this design would look equally good at a wedding reception or for a fun party, suspended over a buffet or drinks table.

Statement mantle arrangement

Mantlepiece arrangements are probably one of my favourite things to decorate; they offer a symmetrical focal point crying out to be decorated. They are also present in many venues so they can provide a wonderful backdrop for any event or celebration. You can make these arrangements huge or small, subtle or impactful – the opportunities are endless. As I like to champion sustainable designs I made this design in chicken wire using a few stems of Gypsophila, Carnations and Roses, for a really delicate but beautiful design. I love asymmetry so this design will be higher on one side, steadily decreasing until you reach the end of the vase and beyond. A wonderful mountain-shaped arrangement that is so pleasing to the eye.

FLOWERS AND FOLIAGE

30 Gypsophila

15 Carnations

15 Roses

OTHER ITEMS

plastic protection

chicken wire measuring length of vase

wire cutters

long and low vase

cable ties

florists' scissors or secateurs

floral water tubes

florists' pot tape

Step 1

Place a bin bag or plastic on the mantlepiece so no damage is caused. Next prepare your structure: take your long and low vase and wrap the chicken wire completely around it. If you want to have a high point at one end, shape the chicken wire to support your stems. Once you have done this, use cable ties to secure the chicken wire in place. Condition the flowers as explained on page 32.

Step 2

Place your chicken-wire covered vase on the mantlepiece and add in the Gypsophila – this can be inserted in small bunches for faster coverage. Steadily graduate the stems shorter and shorter as you move along the chicken wire. It also looks lovely if you have a few stems spilling over the sides to create a bit of a waterfall effect. Starting with the Gypsophila first means that the chicken wire is fully covered and the overall shape of the design is created.

Step 4

We are now ready to add in the Roses and Carnations, which are our focal flowers. For the Roses make sure that all the stems are inserted into small water tubes so they have a water source. The Carnations will last a day without a water supply, so if your display will be up for longer make sure that you put the stems in a water tube too.

Step 3

Once you have added in the Gypsophila, stand back and look at your arrangement to make sure you are happy with the shape.

TIPS AND TRICKS

This arrangement can also be created by arranging a number of different vases of varied heights and sizes filled with water and arranging the stems straight into them. Supplement this with a couple of chicken wire cages at the base of the arrangement to fill in the gaps, and fill them with flowers. This will allow for thirsty flowers to have a larger water supply. This technique would work very well in warmer weather, when your material will need to drink.

The trick to this style of design is to always provide a background first – in this example the background flower is the Gypsophila but any other small-headed flowers or foliage will work equally well.

VARIATIONS

Other focal flowers that will work well in this design are Lilies and Dahlias.

Try making a larger chicken wire arrangement weighted down with some stones in the vase and create a foraged foliage extravaganza, costing you next to nothing – only your time.

Another wonderful and different thing to try is using one variety of flower. Just imagine what you could make with freshly picked Hydrangeas from your garden, massed to create a huge puff of joy. If you do experiment with different flowers, make sure that if they are especially thirsty – like Hydrangeas – you always provide a water source for them. You can always fill your vase with water to aid this process.

Step 5

Place the Carnations and Roses through the arrangement: as always, vary the height and depth of the flowers to ensure your finished design looks three dimensional and interesting. I haven't grouped any of the flowers in this arrangement as I think they look lovely spaced throughout. Remember to leave a few stems quite long to make sure that your focal flowers feature at the tallest part of your arrangement. Once this is done, your arrangement is complete. You can always move the flowers around if you need to as the arrangement is made in chicken wire, but as with all creative design work, don't overthink it too much.

CARNATION

With their multiple petals tightly packed together to form a spiral of loveliness, what's not to like about a Carnation. After falling out of favour in the flower world for some time, they are now experiencing a resurgence. This may be down to the fact that growers are creating the most spectacular varieties, and even offer them as a controversial dyed flower.

My teacher many years ago asked what I loved about a Carnation. My answer was that, like many things in life, people need to really look to see their true beauty. There is beauty in every flower. You just need to take the time to discover it. Carnations are available as a spray variety now as well, which is great to use as a filler flower – and come in a range of colours.

CHRYSANTHEMUM

These wonderful blooms have a very bad reputation because they are generally linked with funerals, so people have a real ingrained prejudice against them. With its knobbly stems – which need careful conditioning – and a very distinctive smell, whatever I say may not change your thoughts on this flower. What I love about the Chrysanthemum is its longevity and concentric perfection. The multiple petals, that start off small in the middle and get larger and larger to form a petal-perfect bloom, cannot be ignored.

Like the Carnation, the bloom Chrysanthemum is becoming more and more popular than its spray counterpart. However, the spray Chrysanthemum should not be discounted – it can provide a great addition cut into sections and spread throughout an arrangement. I do question how these flowers are not more popular – there are very few blooms that look pretty much the same on Day 1 as they do on Day 10 or even 15. Do give these flowers a try in your arrangements and you may be pleasantly surprised.

Carnations, Chrysanthemums and Gladioli

These flowers are now firm favourites of mine because they are cheaper than more fancy flowers, last forever and look great as a one-type arrangement or mixed with other flowers. I wanted to highlight that there is beauty in all flowers, so here are some of my favourite underdogs.

GLADIOLUS

These striking, tall flowers, which can be readily purchased, offer so many opportunities. I feel that they are sometimes overlooked because they look like a thick, long, green twig when they are first bought, and can be quite tricky to arrange. I remember buying two large bunches of Gladioli for a college assessment, and not being able to use them because I hadn't given them the chance to bloom. My teacher said, 'You do realise, Catherine, that every one of the bumps on this stem will bloom in time?' My impatience and naivety in this instance taught me a lesson: some flowers just need time to reach their full potential. So now when I buy armfuls of Gladioli – which are really cheap to purchase when in season – I condition them, place them in fresh water and wait for the magic to happen.

Around Day 5 the tiny bumps start to unravel and, all of a sudden, this fat green stick becomes a flower with multiple blooms. I love the fact that Gladioli can be used when you need to achieve height in an arrangement and cannot access a Delphinium or Snapdragon. My favourite way to enjoy Gladioli is simply placed in a vase, standing tall in all their splendour and offering you days of multi-coloured blooming joy.

DIY
WEDDING

FLOWERS

The flower arrangements are one of the most important aspects of a wedding, often setting the style for everything else. You may think that you will need exotic and unusual blooms to make something really show-stopping – but you can create amazing results with everyday flowers, too. Also, flowers that are in season will always be more cost-effective and easier to source than those that are out of season – so you can achieve much more with the budget available.

This section shows you how you make a bridal bouquet, a buttonhole and a low table arrangement for the venue. Other arrangements in this book, such as garlands (page 112), arches (page 122) and bud vases (page 50), can all easily be adapted for a wedding.

Asymmetrical bridal bouquet

After many years of making wedding flowers, the bridal bouquet is the one item I know I must get right – for many florists this is the item that causes the most stress and angst. Whether it is natural and wild or more structured and contemporary, for me the bouquet style is always the starting point. I am rarely asked to make a bouquet that is a perfect round dome shape – brides seem to prefer a more asymmetric style nowadays, and this more informal style allows for more creativity and the opportunity to design something truly show-stopping. The flower materials you use will be determined by the style of the wedding, and consideration must be given to the type of dress the bride is wearing. I like to think of a bouquet as an accessory to complement the bride and the dress, not take over. I generally make it no bigger than the bride's waist as a guide, and often err on the side of caution and make it on the smaller side – unless the request is for an oversized bouquet, you don't want it to be too heavy or too large to hold. The images you see of bridal bouquets are often very elaborate, with flowers that are not available to many people, but here is a beautiful bouquet using more accessible flowers.

FLOWERS AND FOLIAGE

10 stems of mixed foliage

a few special flowers, such as Stocks, Veronica and a few spray Rose stems

3–5 Roses

3–5 Alstroemeria

3–5 Carnations

3–5 Dahlias

5 Lisianthus

OTHER ITEMS

florists' scissors, secateurs and knife

florists' pot tape

silk ribbon to tie your bouquet

ribbon-cutting scissors

jar or vase

Step 1

Condition the flowers as explained on page 32. Take extra care when removing thorns from Roses – I find using a knife the best tool to do this.

Step 2

Take two pieces of foliage and form a cross by overlapping one stem over the other, holding them loosely in the hand you don't write with. This forms the structure for the bouquet and gives the start of the asymmetrical shape.

Step 3

To achieve a spiral, the rule is to add the material running from left to right in front of the foliage, while everything placed behind the foliage runs from right to left. If you are left-handed you will need to reverse this. As long as the stems are always put in the same direction, either in front or behind, the spiral will still be achieved.

Step 4

Take two Stocks and place one stem in front of your base foliage and one behind as detailed in the previous step.

Step 5

Now add a few of your Roses in varying heights and depths. At this point you need to add in a few flowers that are facing towards you to form a three-dimensional, diamond-like shape.

Step 6

If you are struggling to keep the stems in place, tape them into position by just wrapping a section of florists' pot tape around them. This takes off the pressure of trying to hold them in place, but will still allow you to manipulate the position if you tape the stems loosely enough.

Step 7

Continue to add flowers, mixing them and varying the depth and height, until you are happy with the shape and size of the bouquet. Make sure you place a few blooms on the sides, as it is often photographed from this angle. With this style there is also a front and back so hold on to a few stems, and when you are happy with the front turn your bouquet around and add a few stems in the back using the same technique. Make sure your bride knows there is a front and back – this is normally obvious if there is a trailing ribbon, but to be on the safe side always make sure the bouquet looks lovely on both sides in case your bride forgets which way to hold it.

Step 8

Finish by taping the bouquet in place with pot tape, then trim your stems by cutting them straight across not at an angle. I cut the stems quite short, just long enough for the bride to hold because I really dislike seeing ugly long stems on show – but this is a personal preference.

Step 9

Tie your bouquet with silk ribbon, and place in a jar or vase of water ready for delivery. Make sure the stem ends do not drip water onto the dress by drying them on paper towel.

TIPS AND TRICKS

For the foliage, delicate stems work well and a few trailing vines like Jasmine are a lovely addition. If you forage for foliage you can find some really gorgeous textural materials to add into your bouquet.

Different shaped flowers will help to form the style of the bouquet. Other great flowers to use in this would be Delphiniums and Snapdragons.

For an abundant bouquet I normally use around 50 flower stems and 10 foliage. If you don't want it so flower heavy, use around thirty flower stems and a few foliage stems. Most brides love a variation of flowers in the bouquet, so some of the stems will be very thin and some thicker – the trick is to make sure that you have a balanced mixture. Material choice is key – a bouquet of 50 large-headed Roses would be far too cumbersome.

Buttonhole

At a wedding so much is concentrated on the bride – and rightly so – but what about the groom? Gone are the days when a large Rose and an Ivy leaf will do. I like the groom's buttonhole to be a mini version of the bridal bouquet; a way of linking the bride and groom through flowers as well as union. So, for instance, I like to include a special flower that I have used in the bridal bouquet in the groom's buttonhole – which also acts as a point of difference to other buttonholes worn by the bridal party. Flower choice is key with buttonholes because they will be out of water for a long time – and they will be crushed by hugs and bashed within an inch of their life, so tough flowers are definitely needed. I generally use a spray Rose because they are the perfect size, I find that I can add lots of different elements to them, and they have the added bonus of lasting well out of water. If you need more inspiration, look at my guide on flowers that last well out of water on page 36.

FLOWERS AND FOLIAGE

a few offcuts of foliage from your mixed foliage stems

2 spray Rose stems

2 spray Chrysanthemum; I used Santini variety

1 Alstroemeria

a few dried flower stems for texture

OTHER ITEMS

florists' scissors, secateurs and knife

a few thin silver wires (26-gauge)

wire cutters

florists' stem tape, paper, sticky type

ribbon-cutting scissors

ribbon to tie your buttonhole

pearl head pin

fig. a

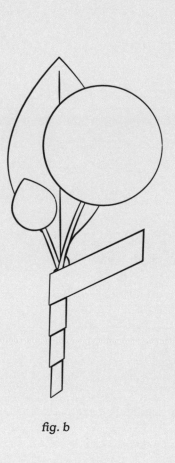

fig. b

fig. c

Step 1

Make sure the flowers are fully conditioned as explained on page 32. They need to have had a really good drink in water for at least 24 hours, because they are going to be out of water for a while.

Step 2

I like to make a support for the buttonhole so it lays nice and flat when pinned onto the lapel. To achieve this, wire a leaf – such as an ivy leaf or any medium-sized leaf with a bit of stalk – with a length of silver wire as explained on page 25 (see fig a, opposite).

Step 3

Cut all the stems you are using to around 7.5 cm (3 in) long initially. You will probably need only three flowers from your selection and a few pieces of foliage. Take your focal flower, which is the spray Rose, and add in the spray Chrysanthemum, maybe a Rose bud and the Alstroemeria. Add some tiny stems of mixed foliage and dried elements if you wish to add interest into your buttonhole.

Step 4

Place your mini bunch onto your wired leaf and tape the buttonhole together with stem tape (see fig b, opposite). You will need to wrap the tape around the buttonhole twice or more to make sure it is fully secured. The back of your buttonhole needs to be flat.

Step 5

Cut the stems a little shorter – around 4 cm (1½ in) as a guide. Finish your buttonhole by tying silk or satin ribbon around the stem tape and then place a pin through the ribbon to allow the buttonhole to be attached.

TIPS AND TRICKS

Deliver buttonholes in water so they remain fresh as long as possible before the big day arrives (see fig. c, opposite).

Use the same technique to make buttonholes for others in the bridal party, and if you have enough stems you can mix the materials to make them look varied and different. You can always try mixing dried and fresh flowers for added texture and interest if you are short of fresh materials.

Low table arrangement

Most weddings will have some type of floral table arrangement at the reception, and I think that low table designs are one of the nicest things to choose. They work well on both long and round tables, and since they are low the guests have the pleasure of enjoying their beauty without any views being obstructed. These arrangements are made in a similar way to the Stand-Out Urn Arrangement on page 96, just on a smaller scale. I like to use a footed bowl for them – because this is shallow it allows for an asymmetric design and for some of the materials to droop over the edge and onto the table for an organic natural look. For a bowl with a 12-cm (4¾-in) opening you don't need too much material, making this very cost effective, too.

FLOWERS AND FOLIAGE

10 stems of mixed foliage; if you forage, you can find some gorgeous textural materials

a few special flowers, such as Veronica, Delphiniums and a few spray Rose stems

5 Roses

1–3 Lilies

3 Carnations

3–5 Lisianthus

3 Alstroemeria

OTHER ITEMS

florists' scissors, secateurs and knife

footed bowl

chicken wire

wire cutters

florists' pot tape

Step 1

Condition the flowers as explained on page 32. Prepare the bowl with the chicken wire as explained on page 22 (see fig. a, opposite).

Step 2

Green up your arrangement by placing the foliage in the chicken wire frame, spaced out and in a loose style. Make sure you have some foliage around the base of the bowl, and a high point and low point to create an asymmetrical shape.

Step 3

Start placing your line flowers (Delphiniums) and your focal flowers (Roses and Lilies) at varying heights. I have used one main focal Lily in this arrangement, but you can use a few more if you wish (see fig. b, opposite). As this arrangement is likely to be seen from all sides, make sure you turn your arrangement and space the focal flowers on both the front and back. The overall height shouldn't be more than around 20 cm (8 in) so guests' views are not obstructed.

Step 4

Add in the Lisianthus and Carnations to fill in gaps in the arrangement and give it some depth. Including a different shaped flower, such as a spray Rose, helps with the style of the arrangement.

Step 5

Continue adding in a variety of your flowers, varying the depth and height. Use spare foliage stems to fill in any gaps. I like to have a bit of a dip in the middle of the arrangement, which suits an asymmetrical design, but a fuller, more rounded shape also looks amazing. Stand away from your arrangement from time to time to check your flower placements.

Step 6

Make a final check from both sides of the arrangement to make sure you are happy with the positioning of your flowers. As this is made in chicken wire you can move the position of the flowers until you have a visually and actual balanced arrangement.

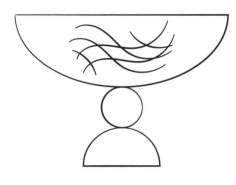

fig. a

fig. b

VARIATIONS

These arrangements are not solely for weddings: they are really versatile so you can make one for a dinner party, or just to sit on a side table or mantle.

Try experimenting with seasonal flowers, this style arrangment looks amazing using spring flowers such as Tulips and Daffodils, which are really good value for money. See page 19 for more seasonal flower inspiration.

See page 19 for more seasonal flower inspiration.

TIPS AND TRICKS

Once you have made one of these arrangements you can use it as a recipe for the others, which will give you a rough idea of how may flowers you may need. You can then purchase a few special stems to add some variation to the arrangements, or have a look in your garden or containers to see what treasures you may find.

LIFE CYCLE OF A ROSE

DAY 1

The Rose is looking tight and pristine, and they look great bunched tightly together.

DAY 5

Now we are starting to see the true beauty of the Rose. Petals are starting to loosen, and if you are lucky enough to have garden Roses, you may be able to see the very centre of the flower – simply gorgeous.

DAY 8

The Rose is starting to fade, petals are beginning to fall and now would be the opportunity to dry them. If this opportunity is missed and you come home one day to a pile of petals, don't throw them away – leave them to dry.

You can try the following with your dried Rose petals:

1   Sprinkle them in bathwater to make a romantic bath.

2   Combine them with herbs, spices and essential oils to create a fragrant pot pourri.

3   Collect lots and scrunch them up to form natural confetti, ready to throw at a wedding.

Roses

Roses are the most wonderful flower. From your supermarket bloom to the most amazing garden Rose, they all have something to offer. Garden Roses give the most beautiful scent and the best thing about them is they are easy to grow. If you are lucky enough to have an outside space you can fill your borders with a few bushes, or if you don't you can grow them in a container. Here are details of the fascinating stages of a Rose – around Day 8 I think they are at their most delicious, at which point you can dry them just before the petals start to fall. The beauty of a Rose can be enjoyed even when it has died and there are many other ways to use them. I also show you a few ways to change the shape of the most ordinary Rose.

CHANGING THE SHAPE OF THE FLOWER

Imagine the scene: you have just come home from the supermarket with a couple of bunches of Roses but the blooms look a bit tight and would look so much better if they were a bit more blousy and open, so what can be done? I have found that blowing into the middle of the Rose, while gently forcing the petals open, will immediately help to loosen the flower.

If you want to go a step further you can reflex the petals to completely change the shape. Starting with the outer petals, gently bend them back from the base of the petal. You must take real care and be gentle because petals are fragile – I have broken off many a petal in the past, as this technique takes a little bit of practise.

After I have transformed my supermarket bunch I love to put them in groups of two or three in bud vases spread around my home, bringing me little snippets of happiness in every room.

About the Author

Catherine Foxwell is a weddings and events florist who lives in South East London with her husband and two children.

Catherine started her floristry journey in 2015 after doing a two-year City and Guilds diploma in floristry course, which allowed her to explore her creativity and learn all the fundamental practices of floristry.

After freelancing in the industry for a year working with a number of top London florists, Catherine decided to set up her own business and Floral Evolution was born.

Catherine has been lucky enough to work with many brands and do lots of amazing weddings over the years. She loves to support up-and-coming businesses, especially ones that are unrepresented in their fields, and runs a free mentorship programme for florists of black and ethnic minority backgrounds to help increase diversity in the industry.

Catherine's love of colour and structure informs her work and she believes that knowing the basics of floristry is a key component to any floristry design. She loves sharing her knowledge and experiences by running workshops and one to one sessions. Her workshops are for new and experienced florists, and for people who just love flowers and want to experience the joy they bring to everyone's lives.

Acknowledgements

Without this sounding like an Oscar winner's speech, there are so many people I would like to thank so here it goes.

First, my wonderful family: my husband Paul who is always the voice of reason and supports me in everything I do. My children, Samuel and Yasmin, who now help me lots with weddings and events. Your ability to remain calm and level-headed helps me to remain calm. I learn lots from you both every day.

To my dear Mum Angela, sisters Joyce and Georgina and my brother Sylvester who have always been there for me and are my constant cheerleaders. I must also mention my nieces and nephews who I don't see as often as I would like as life is so busy, but I really hope to one day do all of your wedding flowers.

To Lesley and Geof, my in-laws, who's love of nature is infectious, are hugely supportive of my business and have the most beautiful garden, which is a constant source of inspiration. And finally, Alison and Gemma, who are a constant support from afar.

I am so lucky to have such a fantastic family and I love you all very much.

To my college teacher Linda Barton. The most wonderful teacher I could have asked to have. The person who allowed me to push the boundaries of traditional floristry, never said I couldn't try something and always encouraged my creativity. You gave me the most unbelievable start to my floristry career, and I will be forever grateful to you.

To all my friends who I have bored with my floristry stories, images and issues. Without being able to talk and express myself on all those occasions I don't know where I would be. And to my lovely florist friends who inspire and support me in my work every single day.

To the wonderful team at Hardie Grant. Eve Marleau, my Commissioning Editor, who first approached me to write this book and made it become a reality; Eila Purvis, my Editor, whose planning and attention to detail is incredible; and Amelia Leuzzi and Bonnie Eichelberger, my designers, who are the creative geniuses behind the design of this book. You have all been the best.

To Kim Lightbody, my photographer, who makes everything look amazing and has such a creative eye. You made everything so easy and the images you have taken for this book are beyond beautiful.

Finally, to my wonderful suppliers, Hoek Flowers, New Covent Garden flower market and Tom Browns wholesale for all the amazing blooms in this book. Also huge thanks to Ros Humphries at The Natural Dyeworks for the beautiful ribbon and Jennifer Kay for the props used in this book.

This has been the most incredible journey and to have all your support to make this happen has been invaluable.

Index

Projects are in *italics*

PUBLISHED IN 2022 BY HARDIE GRANT BOOKS,
AN IMPRINT OF HARDIE GRANT PUBLISHING

HARDIE GRANT BOOKS (LONDON)
5TH & 6TH FLOORS
52–54 SOUTHWARK STREET
LONDON SE1 1UN

HARDIE GRANT BOOKS (MELBOURNE)
BUILDING 1, 658 CHURCH STREET
RICHMOND, VICTORIA 3121

HARDIEGRANTBOOKS.COM

BRITISH LIBRARY CATALOGUING-IN-PUBLICATION DATA.
A CATALOGUE RECORD FOR THIS BOOK IS AVAILABLE FROM THE BRITISH LIBRARY.

FLORAL EVOLUTION
ISBN: 978-1-78488-436-9

10 9 8 7 6 5 4 3 2 1

PUBLISHING DIRECTOR: KAJAL MISTRY
COMMISSIONING EDITOR: EVE MARLEAU
EDITOR: EILA PURVIS
DESIGN AND ART DIRECTION:
AMELIA LEUZZI
& BONNIE EICHELBERGER
ILLUSTRATIONS: BONNIE EICHELBERGER
PHOTOGRAPHER: KIM LIGHTBODY
COPY-EDITOR: MARIE CLAYTON
PROOFREADER: GILLIAN HASLAM
INDEXER: CATHY HEATH
PRODUCTION CONTROLLER: KATIE JARVIS

COLOUR REPRODUCTION BY P2D
PRINTED AND BOUND IN CHINA